MW01048861

Hero of the Pre-War Olympiads Grandmaster Vladimirs Petrovs

Dmitry Kryakvin and Galina Petrova-Matisa

Hero of the Pre-War Olympiads: Grandmaster Vladimirs Petrovs
Authors: Dmitry Kryakvin and Galina Petrova-Matisa

Translated from the Russian by Alexei Zakharov
Chess editor: Grigory Baranov
Typesetting by Andrei Elkov
Front cover photo dates to 1929

Follow us on Twitter: @ilan_ruby
www.elkandruby.com
ISBN 978-5-6047849-0-7 (paperback), 978-5-6047849-1-4 (hardback)

Contents

Index of Games

33	G. Stahlberg	V. Petrovs	Fragment	1939
34	V. Petrovs	V. Mikenas	Fragment	1939
35	V. Petrovs	A. Kotov	Fragment	1940
36	A. Konstantinopolsky	V. Petrovs	Caro-Kann Defense	1940
37	V. Petrovs	A. Lilienthal	Fragment	1940
38	M. Botvinnik	V. Petrovs	Fragment	1940
39	V. Petrovs	I. Boleslavsky	Fragment	1940
40	V. Smyslov	V. Petrovs	Fragment	1940
41	V. Petrovs	G. Levenfish	King's Indian Defense	1940
42	V. Petrovs	G. Lisitsin	Fragment	1940
43	V. Petrovs	M. Stolberg	Fragment	1940
44	V. Petrovs	V. Makogonov	Fragment	1940
45	P. Keres	V. Petrovs	King's Gambit	1940
46	Z. Solmanis	V. Petrovs	Four Knights Defense	1940
47	V. Petrovs	B. Goldenov	Fragment	1941
48	A. Chistiakov	V. Petrovs	Sicilian Defense	1941
49	V. Mikenas	V. Petrovs	Fragment	1942
50	V. Ragozin	V. Petrovs	Fragment	1942
51	V. Petrovs	I. Boleslavsky	Fragment	1942
52	V. Petrovs	G. Ilivitsky	Fragment	1942

Preface by Vladimir Dedkov

Time progresses implacably, following laws known only unto itself. And we divide it into segments based on what we were doing at the time. Sometimes, minutes drag on for ages, adding up to excruciating hours, days, years. And when it's all quiet around you, decades can pass by very quickly. This is how time passed for the members of our family, the descendants of Vladimirs Mikhailovich Petrovs, who was born in Riga in 1908. And now, it's 2013, the 105th anniversary of his birth...

Five years have passed since the publication of the book *A Star Prematurely Extinguished* (2008), my grandmother's memories of my grandfather Vladimirs Petrovs. We, her grandchildren, only started to decipher her notes on newspaper scraps, tissue paper and even cigarette packs after her death.

Galina Mikhailovna Petrova-Matisa, a strict but fair and loving grandmother, very principled in many respects, dedicated her life to the rehabilitation of her first husband and the search for his grave.

My mother, who died 28 years ago, Petrovs' only child, Marina Vladimirovna, was just two-and-a-half years old when my grandfather left to play in the semi-final of the 13th Soviet Championship in 1941. This was the last time she ever saw her father. Did she remember the image of her father, his eyes full with endless love? It's hard to say. But she carried the certainty that he was innocent throughout her life.

It's been 70 years since my grandfather died. Or was killed? His nameless grave has never seen any flowers, and there was no memorial service... Everything seems to indicate that my grandfather died a non-violent death – pneumonia, which he contracted during the transfer to the camp. He was taken off the train with a high fever somewhere around Kotlas. It's unlikely that he was "dispatched", as my grandmother used to say, in a jail for espionage. She did suspect that, since, according to documents, Petrovs' name was never recorded in any camp prisoner lists. Thus, time after time, she became increasingly insistent, asking, demanding where possible, even begging to be told the truth about her husband's death.

At the first interrogation, on the day of his arrest, when asked to provide a list of people who could act as character witnesses for him, my grandfather listed the names of people he thought close to him. All of them were subpoenaed, and they all testified against him!

We shouldn't blame any of them. Ideologically, they were probably cut from an entirely different cloth than my grandfather, who was born and grew up in bourgeois Latvia. They could sincerely have believed that they were right. Or they could have been afraid for themselves and their relatives.

This was proved in 1959, when Vladimirs Petrovs' case went to a retrial – my mother sent a request for his rehabilitation after Stalin's death. Everyone thought back then that the officials just sent a formal reply – "not subject to rehabilitation", and that's all. However, it turns out that there was a full-blown archival investigation, overseen by supervisors from the state security organs. Everyone was interrogated once again, except for two witnesses who had already died, and they even found three more acquaintances of my grandfather from his inner circle. Everyone, except one woman, confirmed they believed their old testimonies were correct, but couldn't repeat them because it had happened too long ago.

And that's even though the testimonies themselves were laughable, especially by modern standards:

– He repeatedly "drew comparisons between life in the USSR and Western Europe, in favor of the latter…"

– At the start of the Great Patriotic War *[After Germany invaded the Soviet Union]*, he said, "There was a lot of talk in the USSR about preparing for the war, but there was actually next to no preparation. As a result, the army was disorganized and its military action very poorly run."

– Concerning the people of the Baltic republics and the Bessarabian SSR, he said that the citizens of those republics "had no intention to ally with Russia."

And here's testimony of some person who didn't even quote my grandfather directly: "Petrovs' words gave me the feeling that he regretted his decision to return from Argentina, where he had taken part in a chess tournament. I was under the impression that Petrovs wouldn't mind leaving the Soviet Union altogether."

My grandfather refused to plead guilty and rejected all the witnesses' testimonies during questioning. That's probably why he was sentenced to the camps for 10 years, not 8, as was recommended by the senior investigator of the Moscow Oblast NKVD Department.

If not for tuberculosis lesions in his upper lung, my grandfather would have probably served his ten years for so-called "anti-Soviet propaganda" and would have continued to play his beloved chess. And, what's more, his loving wife and daughter would have seen him again. Maybe he would even have lived long enough to see his grandchildren… But, as they say, history does not know the subjunctive mood, and so, only one thing remains for us: using what little that was left to remember his name and cherish his blessed memory.

Is there any kind of pattern in what happened to Vladimirs Mikhailovich Petrovs? I think that there is! It was foretold by the Latvian soothsayer and photographer Eizens Finks, when my grandfather went to his studio to have his photo taken shortly before leaving for Argentina: he said that his star was shining bright, but it would soon fade. The pattern continues in what happened with my grandmother's family, the descendants of a noble family from Chernigov. We find the pattern everywhere. Even in the fact that my small self-published book of my grandmother's personal memories, featuring zero chess diagrams, broke down the wall of obscurity surrounding the name of Grandmaster Vladimirs Mikhailovich Petrovs – his life and legacy attracted the interest of chess players and fans in both Latvia and Russia.

Six years have passed since my first meeting with Alexei Shirov – the first person to respond to the request to help publish the book about my grandfather. His contribution to restoring my grandfather's blessed memory was invaluable. I am very grateful to him! Thanks to him for publishing the Russian version of the book you are now holding with modern analysis of my grandfather's games as well.

Dmitry Kryakvin called the third part of his 2012 research on my grandfather's last tournaments "The Victim of the Soviet Moloch". Is this close to the truth? In part, yes. Retracing Vladimirs Mikhailovich Petrovs' life and looking through case files, we, his descendants, have formed an opinion that he was a victim of unfortunate circumstances first and foremost. That's why we decided to name the last chapter in Dmitry's part of this book "A Victim of Circumstances".

Part I: Selected Games and Career, by Dmitry Kryakvin (2013)

Vladimirs Petrovs is one of the most enigmatic and tragic figures in chess history. His name was struck out of chess literature for decades. His games and biography are largely unknown to the public – even though Petrovs defeated Alekhine, Fine, Reshevsky, Boleslavsky and many other famous players of the past, gained prizes at many supertournaments and won some outright, as well as performing strongly on first board at chess Olympiads.

The Leading Scorer of the Latvian Team

The idea of writing what was originally a series of articles came up after a long argument with one of my friends who knew chess history very well. My friend was of the opinion that we tend to overestimate the strength of past masters, especially if they are our compatriots – we speculate and read too much into their biography. Take Klaus Junge, for instance – a talented German chess player who perished during World War II. Suddenly, someone shows interest in his games, and he quickly gets covered by myths and legends. He allegedly had a huge plus score against Alekhine, and he was also the one who developed the Botvinnik System, with the Patriarch merely copying his analysis, and had he stayed alive, he would have become the sixth world champion, destroying all the Soviet players in the match tournament. Or, if the article is written by someone who suffered under Soviet rule, it's usually colored in emotional black and bright red. Or, say, let's take some provincial master who played well in the last century: in the eyes of his fellow townsmen, he was a genius and would surely have won the Soviet Championship, had it not been the sinister hand of the Kremlin

A young Vladimirs Petrovs, 1924

stopping him, forcing him to lose to some KGB-backed grandmaster at a crucial moment. Well, he drank a bit and behaved somewhat seditiously, the local sports committee disliked him for that, didn't allow him to go abroad for tournaments, he didn't get called up to the Russian SFSR team, even though he was at least as talented as Karpov! In other words, they nipped a future world champion in the bud...

My deliberations about Petrovs' strength and talent were met with the same kind of skepticism. What was his score in the Soviet Championship? Minus one? How many Soviet masters had a plus score in the Soviet Championships but never became grandmasters? Don't you remember Keres checkmating him in the opening, haven't you read *Paul Keres Chess University*? These arguments could only be countered with facts, and so, to try to convince my incredulous friend, I had to analyze dozens of games played by Vladimirs Petrovs. As I studied the books and articles about the Latvian grandmaster, I noticed that the annotations of his games were rather short and shallow, and it was hard to use them as proof of Petrovs' strength. Dates and events are sometimes mixed up. But we shouldn't blame the authors: after all, they did bring to light the appalling story that happened to one of the most talented players of the pre-war period. I would like

to share my thoughts from this research. So, dear readers, let's dive into the career of Grandmaster Vladimirs Petrovs!

Petrovs took up chess at the age of 13 and achieved success relatively quickly. At the age of 15, he won a secondary tournament of the first Latvian Congress, and two years later, he shared 2nd–3rd places in the main tournament. His games against Latvian masters Matisons and Apsenieks were hard-fought battles, and in 1925, Petrovs won the Riga Championship in brilliant style, two points ahead of the runner-up. After these successes, the young player was invited to the Latvian national team to compete at the Hague Olympiad (1928).

The novice wasn't trusted with a high board – he played board 3 – and the line-up of his opponents was rather modest, including only a few masters. His overall score was also quite modest, 8.5/16. The Olympiad consisted of 17 rounds, and Petrovs rested only once, after losing to Steiner. His only substantial achievement was his win against Poland's Kazimierz Makarczyk, one of the players featured in Evgeny Gik's book *Funny Stories from Chess Players' Lives*. The Polish team was rather strong, featuring Akiba Rubinstein and Savielly Tartakower (who hadn't settled in France yet). In 1930, Poland would win the Olympiad, and Makarczyk would later earn the master's title.

Game 1

V. Petrovs – K. Makarczyk
The Hague 1928, round 9
(Latvia – Poland)
Queen's Gambit Declined

1.d4 d5 2.c4 e6 3.♘f3 ♘f6 4.♗g5
♗e7 5.♘c3 0-0 6.e3 ♘bd7 7.♖c1 c6
8.♕c2 ♘e4 9.♗xe7 ♕xe7 10.♘xe4
dxe4 11.♘d2 f5 12.c5 e5 13.♗e2
exd4 14.♕c4+ ♔h8 15.♕xd4 ♖d8
16.♘b3 ♘b6 17.♕c3 ♘d5 18.♕c4
f4 19.0-0

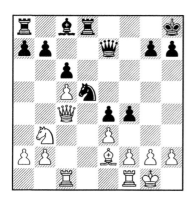

White's opening play was quite
poor and he got under attack. Now
black could win an exchange and the
game with 19...f3 20.gxf3 ♗h3, but this
simple resource was left unnoticed.

**19...♖f8? 20.exf4 ♖xf4 21.♘d4
♕g5?!**

In the post-mortem analysis, the
opponents found a pretty line 21...
e3!, and if 22.fxe3?, then 22...♘xe3!
23.♘xc6 ♕g5! 24.♕e4 ♗f5!, and
black wins.

22.♕b3 ♕e5?!

22...e3 still worked: 23.♘f3 (not
23.fxe3 ♘xe3) 23...exf2+ 24.♔h1

(24.♖xf2 ♖xf3 loses) 24...♕e7
25.♖xf2 ♗g4 with a big advantage
for black. Now, however, all three
results become possible.

**23.♖cd1 ♖b8 24.♕g3 ♗d7
25.♗c4 ♖bf8**

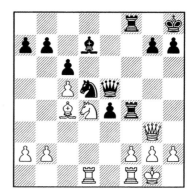

Petrovs had gradually outplayed
his opponent, and 26.♘e2 forced a
transition to a favorable endgame.
However, there followed

26.♗xd5?

ChessBase gave this move an
exclamation mark, but it's a mistake
– both by the players and the
commentator.

26...cxd5?

A mistake in return. Black could
have cheekily taken the bishop with
26...♕xd5!; white has two pawns en
prise, and 27.♘e2 is met with 27...
♖xf2, with black still having an extra
pawn. After Makarczyk's mistake,
Petrovs forces a queen exchange
in the best possible situation and
tightens his positional grip on black's
throat.

**27.♘e2 ♖4f5 28.♕xe5 ♖xe5
29.♘c3 ♗c6 30.b4 ♖d8 31.♖d4**

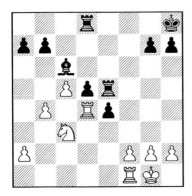

31...♔g8 32.♖fd1 e3 33.fxe3 ♖xe3 34.♘xd5 ♗xd5 35.♖xd5 ♖xd5 36.♖xd5, and white showed good technique in converting his extra pawn. The game is uneven, but we should bear in mind that Vladimirs Petrovs was only 19 years old – a small kid by the standards of the time, and it was his first tournament abroad. Still, I don't want to imagine what the great Akiba could have said to the Polish player after the game.

Two years later, however, the novice of the Latvian team had improved considerably. He played board 3 again, but this time, he performed as an apex predator, scoring 11/17 and not missing a single game, even though he faced such strong players as Winter, Eliskases, Takacs, Landau, Ahues, Stahlberg, Tartakower and Frank Marshall himself! Petrovs made a flying start – 4.5/5 – and he again won an important game in the match against Poland. This time, the Riga player took down the

author of *The Hypermodern Game of Chess.*

Game 2
S. Tartakower – V. Petrovs
Hamburg 1930, round 3
(Poland – Latvia)
Queen's Pawn Game

1.d4 ♘f6 2.g3 d5 3.♗g2 e6 4.♘f3 c5 5.0-0 ♘c6 6.b3 cxd4 7.♘xd4 ♗c5 8.♗b2 ♕b6 9.e3 0-0

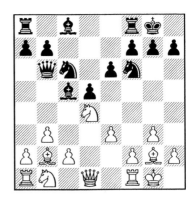

The grandmaster of chess journalism was rather creative in his opening play: here, 10.♘xc6 bxc6 11.♗xf6 gxf6 seems logical. To be honest, I can't understand why that position has been evaluated in white's favor. Because he can give a check? I think that Petrovs would have gladly played that position as black, relying on the potential of his bishop pair. White probably should play 12.♘c3 here (both 12.♕g4+ ♔h8 13.♕h4 ♕d8 14.c4 f5 and 12.c4 d4 pose no trouble for black) 12...♗e7 13.♘a4 with the subsequent c4, trying to fix the pawn structure in the center, but this would be a struggle. Savielly Grigorievich, however, decided to push the black pieces back with a temporary knight sacrifice, but he forgot that winning the queen did not mean winning the game.

10.♘c3?! ♗xd4! 11.♘a4?

And this is the decisive mistake. White should have given up the pawn, 11.exd4 ♕xd4 12.♘a4, for some serious compensation. Black's queenside is underdeveloped, white is planning to break in the center with c2-c4, and the knight will target c5 after the queen exchange.

11...♗xb2!

Petrovs bravely sacrifices his queen for three minor pieces and a pawn, correctly surmising that black's compensation was more than enough.

12.♘xb6 axb6 13.♖b1 ♖xa2

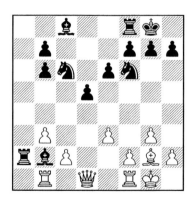

14.c4

14.♕d2 ♗e5 changes nothing – white's position is absolutely hopeless. His queen is powerless

against the onslaught of black pieces that crush the defenseless white pawns. The white army is paralyzed, and he can only wait for the inevitable.

14...♗e5 15.♕c1 ♘e4 16.♗xe4 dxe4 17.b4 ♗f6 18.♕d1 ♘e5 19.♕b3 ♖e2 20.♖bd1 ♘f3+ 21.♔g2 ♖b2 22.♕a4 ♘d2. New material losses are inevitable, and white soon resigned. This was Petrovs' first published game to become famous.

Alas, Petrovs' successful streak soon broke. In round 6, he was checkmated by Marshall in 17 moves, and then lost with white in the match against Romania. However, the leading scorer of the Latvian team didn't lose heart; the draws against the strong Stahlberg and Ahues helped him to overcome the crisis and come out of the dive. Petrovs defeated Master Salo Landau with white, and, despite an unnecessary loss against Denmark, achieved a +5 score with a winning streak at the finish. A great result! Sometimes the Latvian played rather poorly in the opening, getting unpleasant positions – probably because of his lack of experience. But Petrovs' positional play was very competent even back then – he didn't create unnecessary weaknesses and sometimes outplayed his opponents out of nowhere! He was very strong in technical endgames, playing to the very end with an iron hand.

Game 3

V. Petrovs – S. Landau

Hamburg 1930, round 11
(Latvia – Netherlands)

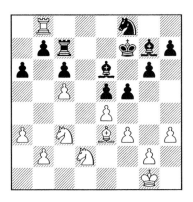

Vladimirs Petrovs' opponent in this game was the Dutch master Salo Landau, a well-known theoretician who later worked as Alexander Alekhine's second in his match against Max Euwe in 1935. Landau's fate was no less tragic than Petrovs': he perished in a Nazi deathcamp, probably in 1944, as did his wife and young daughter. The endgame of this encounter between the victims of Stalin's and Hitler's regimes became a training example. The white rook is active, but the black e6 bishop reigns supreme over the light squares, and this seems to give black enough compensation. Landau probably thought that his position was safe, and so he made a grave positional mistake.

25...f4?

Black removes the tension in the center and basically gives up any chances of counterplay along the d-file. 25...♖d7 was very strong, threatening to win a piece with f5-f4.

26.♗f2 ♗f6?

Landau still doesn't sense danger. It was not too late to play ♖d7 or immediately start a pawn attack on the kingside: 26...g5 27.♔f1 h5 28.b4 ♖d7 29.♔e2 g4 30.hxg4 hxg4 31.♞a4 ♖c7, intending to play g4-g3 and then put the knight on h4. Now white's plan is rather simple: the king goes to the center, the knight goes to c4 through b6, the bishop goes to c3, and black loses because of numerous weaknesses – the b7 and e5 pawns and d6 square.

27.♔f1 ♞d7 28.♖a8 ♞f8 29.♖a7! g5 30.b4 ♞g6 31.♞a4 ♞e7 32.♞b6

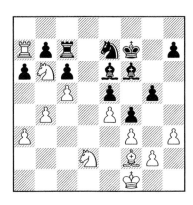

Black's position is already difficult, but the knight trade offered by the Dutch player only leads to a quicker defeat.

32...♞c8 33.♞xc8 ♗xc8 34.♞c4 ♔e7 35.♖a8 ♔d8 36.♖b8 ♔e7 37.♞d6 ♗e6

White can already take the b7 pawn, but Petrovs doesn't hurry: the pawn isn't going anywhere. He calmly transfers his bishop to c3.

38.♗e1 h5 39.♗c3 g4 40.hxg4 hxg4 41.♔e2 g3

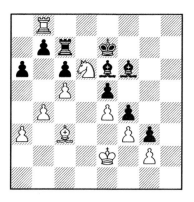

Black has fixed the g2 pawn and is ready to meet the pawn grab 42.♘xb7 with 42...♖c8 – the rooks are exchanged, and white will face a lot of technical difficulties while converting his material advantage. Therefore, white sets a small trap first. Trying to win "with less effort", as Capablanca taught.

42.♖e8+ ♔d7 43.♗b2 ♗g7?

The correct 43...♗f7 forced white to retreat with the rook and try to strengthen his queenside – get the king there and push the pawns. Now, however, black loses immediately: as soon as the rook moves away, there's no defense against the crushing ♘e8!

44.♖b8 ♔e7 45.♘e8 ♗c4+ 46.♔e1 ♖d7 47.♘xg7 ♖d3 48.♘f5+ ♔e6 49.♖e8+ ♔d7 50.♖e7+ ♔d8 51.♗xe5. Black resigned. Exquisite technique by white!

Vladimirs Petrovs' credentials and playing strength became so great that he even challenged for the first board in the Latvian team. Of course, this made the older generation unhappy, especially the team leader, Master Fricis Apsenieks. Petrovs wanted to play board 1 at the Prague 1931 Olympiad, to face Alekhine and other strong grandmasters, but again, he had to settle for board 3 – and took the gold for that board with an 11.5/16 score! Petrovs lost to masters Thomas and Rejfir, drew against Noteboom, Przepiorka and Kmoch, and the only well-known player he defeated was Horowitz, but in round 3, he won a game where he implemented a rather familiar plan!

Game 4
L. Hansen – V. Petrovs
Prague 1931, round 3
(Norway – Latvia)
Sicilian Defense

1.e4 c5 2.♘f3 ♘c6 3.d4 cxd4 4.♘xd4 ♘f6 5.♘c3 d6 6.♗e2 g6 7.0-0 ♗g7 8.♗e3 0-0 9.♘b3 ♘e5 10.f3 ♗e6 11.♘d5 ♖c8 12.♘xf6+ ♗xf6 13.♗d4

White threatens f3-f4-f5, so black's reaction is completely logical.

13... g5! 14.c3

What now? The most logical and obvious plan is a6-b5, then ♗c4 — the standard Sicilian queenside play. Petrovs, however, chooses another path.

14...♔h8

Why does he play this?

15.♘c1

The Norwegian player plays logically – prepares to trade his poor b3 knight for the strong black one on e5.

15...♖g8! 16.♘d3 ♛a5 17.♛e1 ♖g7 18.♛f2 ♖cg8!

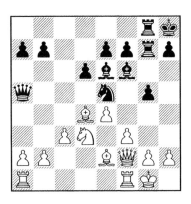

Here's the thing! Twelve years before Bobby Fischer was born, Vladimirs Petrovs paradoxically doubles rooks along the closed g-file (though Paul Morphy was the first to use this technique)! Black's threats are obvious, and Hansen is forced to calculate lines.

19.g4!?

A logical move made to limit the activity of black's rooks. Taking the a7 pawn is dangerous: 19.♘xe5 ♗xe5 20.♗xa7 g4! 21.♛b6 gxf3 22.♗xf3 ♛a4 23.♛xb7 ♗c8 24.♛b6 ♖xg2+ 25.♗xg2 ♛xe4 26.♗f2 ♗b7, and black's attack on the long diagonal is most likely decisive.

19...h5 20.♗xe5

20.♘xe5!? ♗xe5 21.♗xa7 hxg4 22.fxg4 ♖h7 23.♗d4 f6 24.♗xe5 ♛xe5 25.♛g3 was worth considering: black has decent compensation, but a pawn is a pawn.

20...♗xe5   21.♘xe5   ♛xe5 22.♛g3?

A grave mistake. White is ready for big positional concessions to avoid his opponent's attack and transpose into an ending, but this is precisely what Petrovs was expecting. The correct move was 22.♛xa7 hxg4 23.fxg4 ♖h7 (23...♛xe4 24.♗f3 is dangerous – black can lose the b7 pawn) 24.♛d4 ♖h4 25.♛xe5+ dxe5 26.♖f2 ♔g7 27.♖g2 ♖d8 with a complicated endgame; black, again, has good compensation for the pawn.

22...♛xg3+   23.hxg3   hxg4 24.fxg4 ♖h7

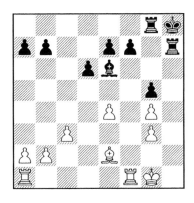

There's a technical endgame on the board. Due to the threat of black rooks invading along the h-file, white is forced to allow the black king to get to e5, and after that, he can't hold his numerous pawn weaknesses.

25.♔g2 ♔g7 26.♖h1 ♖xh1 27.♖xh1 ♔f6 28.♖d1 ♔e5 29.♗f3 ♖c8 30.a3 a5 31.♔f2 b5 32.♖d4 ♗b3!

The finishing touch. With his two last moves, Petrovs prevents any white activity on the kingside, the b2 pawn is fixed, and the white pawns fall, one after another.

33.♔e3 ♖h8 34.♗e2 ♖h2 35.a4 bxa4 36.♖d2 ♖h1 37.c4 e6 38.c5 dxc5 39.♖d7 ♖b1 40.♖a7 ♖xb2 41.♖xa5 ♔d6 42.e5+ ♔c6 43.♖a8 c4

White resigned. A great win! As you can see, the eleventh world champion spent a lot of time studying the games of past masters.

Vladimirs continued to improve in leaps and bounds: he scored 13/13 in his qualifying group at the 3rd Latvian Chess Congress, and then convincingly defeated Feigins, the winner of the second qualifying group, in a match – 5.5–2.5. Still, his first individual international tournament, Moravska Ostrava 1933, was not a success. The 12-player tournament included such famous names as Ernst Grunfeld (the inventor of the very popular defense), Vasja Pirc (the inventor of the somewhat less popular defense), Josef Rejfir, Erich Eliskases, Jan Foltys and Lajos Steiner. On occasions, the Latvian (who had already been unofficially awarded the master's title – back then, this title reflected the player's authority among his colleagues and chess connoisseurs, not points, Elo ratings or norms) played rather well, for instance, his play against Grunfeld was very subtle. But he was let down by his technique and unfortunate blunders in time trouble.

Game 5
K. Gilg – V. Petrovs
Moravska Ostrava 1933

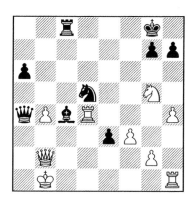

Black had completely outplayed his opponent, and Gilg would have probably just resigned after 32...♘xb4, but there followed

32...♗a2+?? 33.♕xa2

Oh, the horror! The knight is pinned!

33...♕xa2+ 34.♔xa2 ♘c3+ 35.♔b2

Black resigned. Petrovs scored only 5/11 – way below his expected result.

After that, Vladimirs Petrovs had to settle for board 2 at the Folkestone 1933 Olympiad. Not the coveted first board, but at least not the third! The grandmaster's widow wrote in her book *A Star Prematurely Extinguished* that the atmosphere in the Latvian team was not always healthy. Once, the captain of the Latvian team miscalculated the amount of money needed, and the players had to spend the night before the last round literally on the street. Petrovs and Apsenieks publicly criticized each other and blamed each other for the team's setbacks. In Folkestone, Petrovs started with 3/3, but then his performance was uncharacteristically pallid, and he scored 7.5/14 overall. Even though the Riga player defeated Treybal and Thomas and drew with Stoltz, he lost way too many games – not only to Steiner, Eliskases and the super-heavyweight Reuben Fine, but to some less known players, too.

The question of the leadership of the Latvian national chess team remained open. The first Latvian Championship was played in 1934, with Petrovs and Apsenieks sharing first place. The regulations stated that they had to play a deciding match, but the rivals came to a gentlemen's agreement: Fricis would get the substantial money prize and the champion's title, and Vladimirs would get the right to play board 1 at the next Olympiad. Since then, Vladimirs played board 1 for Latvia at all the Olympiads until Latvia was annexed by the Soviet Union, and he also convincingly won all the subsequent national championships! Such talks, however, were a truly unique occurrence and unimaginable today.

In 1934, an important event was held in Riga: a match between Spielmann and Petrovs. The famous maestro Spielmann wasn't exactly a spring chicken (he was 50 years old), and the incredible chess successes of his youth were already in the distant past. The author of *The Art of Sacrifice in Chess* was plagued by poor results, he desperately tried to switch to a more positional style and learn classical openings theory; he even published a repentant article called "At the Death Bed of the Dying King's Gambit". Alas, this didn't help that much, and a year later, Spielmann would fare poorly in Moscow, losing to Botvinnik in 13 moves! All in all, it seemed that Petrovs could successfully handle his illustrious opponent. The beginning of the match gave a lot of hope to the local fans.

Game 6
R. Spielmann – V. Petrovs
Riga 1934 (game 1)

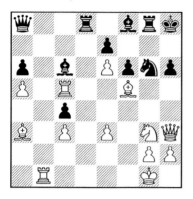

The Austrian master has played very well in this first game and completely outmaneuvered the local player. White has an extra pawn on e6, and the black bishop on f8 is out of play – essentially, white thus has an extra piece. Nevertheless, black is still counting on his counter-attack along the long diagonal in mutual time trouble.

33.♕h5

The simplest continuation was 33.♖f1 ♖d2 34.e4 ♖c2 35.♕h5: black's threats are repelled, and his position is critical. Spielmann, however, shows his disregard for black's possible counterplay. Not a good choice...

33...♖d2! 34.♗xg6?

It still wasn't too late to trade the opponent's active rook with 34.♖b2! ♖xb2 35.♗xb2 ♘e5 36.♕e2, and white has every chance of winning. Now, however, Petrovs executes a beautiful combination despite having little time left on the clock.

34...♖xg2+ 35.♔f1 ♗f3 36.♕f5?

The last mistake. The black queen could have been distracted with 36.♖c8 ♕xc8 37.♕xf3 ♖a2 38.♗e4, with an incredibly complicated position. After the game move, black wins by force.

36...♖xg6! 37.♕xg6 ♗e2+

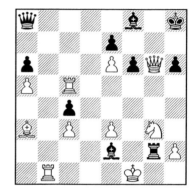

It turns out that the bishop is taboo because of a mate in two, and so the black queen invades the opponent's camp.

38.♔e1 ♕f3! 39.♕f5 ♕xe3 40.♗c1 ♕g1+ 41.♘f1 ♗g4! White resigns.

An elegant finishing touch. White either gets checkmated or loses his queen, and so Petrovs took the lead in the match, 1–0.

Spielmann later seized the initiative, first winning back, and then taking a 3.5–2.5 lead after game 6. The match could have ended prematurely in game 7, but the famous guest missed an opportunity to win a piece, and then too quickly agreed to a draw in the endgame. Down 4–3, Petrovs had to win the last game on demand. But after getting a promising endgame, Vladimirs played indecisively and allowed his opponent to escape.

Game 7
V. Petrovs – R. Spielmann
Riga 1934 (game 8)

White has a clear positional advantage. His strong knight cramps black's position, the rooks are active, and the pawn structure is conducive for a possible minority attack. The only possible counterplay for black is to try to push e6-e5. Therefore, the classical recipe for white in this position is 31.f4! with the subsequent ♔f3, and then, when black's activity is limited, white can prepare a pawn break on either flank. However, Petrovs played too rashly and overlooked a strong reply from his opponent.

31.b4?! b5! 32.♔f2 ♘c4

The black knight gets to c4, and now white has to defend the e3 pawn and doesn't have enough time to attack the opponent's queenside pawn weaknesses.

33.a4

33.♖d3 ♘b2 34.♖b3 ♘c4 35.f4 f6 gives white nothing: black will still play e6-e5.

33...♘b2   34.♖d2   ♘xa4 35.♘xa4?!

White retained some small chances of winning with 35.♘b3 e5 36.♖xc6, but the Latvian was already demoralized and decided to stop fighting.

35...bxa4 36.♖a2 e5 37.dxe5 ♖xe5 38.♖xc6 a5 with a draw. Spielmann therefore won the match in a tense struggle. Of course, scoring 3.5/8 against a grandmaster who was unquestionably a world top-10 player in the 1920s was a good result. But Petrovs obviously wanted more!

At the Warsaw 1935 Olympiad, Petrovs was the first board, leader and captain of the Latvian team. It was his first competition where he faced many of the greatest stars of the chess world: Paul Keres, Salo Flohr, Reuben Fine, Alexander Alekhine and a dozen strong masters. The Latvian leader scored 10.5/19, playing without a rest. Petrovs' teammates considered this a brilliant success: he essentially scored +2 in a supertournament! The Latvian team, inspired by his success, took 9th place – a great achievement for the Baltic team. However, Petrovs was critical of his own performance in a letter to his wife, saying that he should have scored more – he lamented an upsetting loss to Keres and the refusal of Fine's draw offer.

Game 8
V. Petrovs – R. Fine
Warsaw 1935, round 8
(Latvia – USA)
Queen's Gambit Declined

1.d4 d5 2.♘f3 ♘f6 3.c4 e6 4.♗g5 ♘bd7 5.e3 ♗e7 6.♘c3 0-0 7.♖c1 c6 8.♕c2 a6 9.cxd5 exd5 10.♗d3 h6 11.♗h4 c5 12.dxc5 ♘xc5 13.0-0 ♗e6 14.♘d4 ♖c8 15.♖fd1 b5 16.a3 ♘e8 17.♗xe7 ♕xe7

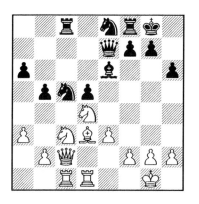

In this position, the American grandmaster, who always had a strong sense of danger, offered a draw. Petrovs was correct in refusing the draw, but his subsequent play was far from ideal.

18.b4?!

Vladimirs hadn't learned his lesson from the Spielmann game and significantly weakened the c4 square, which gave black good compensation for his isolated queen's pawn. In addition to the standard

18.♕e2 ♘d6 19.♗b1, white had a pretty combination: 18.♗f5! ♘f6 (18...♘d6 loses to 19.♘xd5! ♗xd5 20.♗xc8 ♖xc8 21.♘f5 ♘xf5 22.♖xd5) 19.♘xe6 fxe6 20.♘xd5 ♘xd5 21.♖xd5 ♖xf5 (21...exd5 22.♗xc8 ♖xc8 23.b4) 22.♖xf5 exf5 23.b4 f4 24.bxc5 fxe3 25.♕b3+, with an extra pawn.

18...♘a4!

Reuben Fine plays precisely: he doesn't need to trade the opponent's light-squared bishop, getting the knight to the coveted c4 square is much more important than that! Perhaps Petrovs counted on 18...♘xd3? 19.♕xd3 ♘d6 20.♘b3 ♘c4 21.♘xd5 ♗xd5 22.♕xd5 ♘xa3 23.♘c5, with domination for the white pieces.

19.♕d2 ♘xc3 20.♖xc3 ♘d6 21.♘b3

White should have tolerated the pesky knight: 21.♖dc1! ♘c4 22.♕d1, gradually preparing to get rid of it. Petrovs decided to resolve the problem cardinally and got a worse position.

21...♘c4 22.♗xc4 dxc4 23.♘d4 ♕f6 24.♕e2 ♖fd8

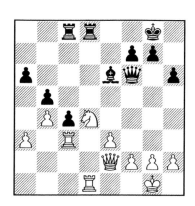

Black's position is very good. He has a strong protected passed pawn on c4, and his bishop, which was rather puny just a few moves ago, would soon dominate the position. White had to quickly build barricades on light squares with f3 and h3, but after the sharp

25.f4? ♗d5 26.♖d2 ♗e4

Fine easily converted his advantage.

The public indeed considered Petrovs' overall result a great success. Yes, he lost to Alekhine, Fine and Flohr, and so what? Together with Euwe, Capablanca, Botvinnik, Lasker and Reshevsky, those three were the strongest grandmasters of the world, played very strongly even

Latvia vs. Lithuania, first round of the Chess Olympiad in Warsaw, August 1935. Fricis Apsenieks is playing on board two

from the modern point of view, and chess fans of the 1930s considered them practically invincible. And the 19 year-old Paul Keres became the revelation of the Olympiad and immediately joined the ranks of the world chess elite. Yet Petrovs scored +6 against other top players!

The Latvian maestro received an invitation to a star-studded event in Podebrady, Czechoslovakia (1936). The list of participants included Alexander Alekhine, who wanted to regain his form before the return match against Euwe, Jan Foltys, Vasja Pirc, Gideon Stahlberg, Erich Eliskases, Lajos Steiner, Karel Opocensky, Karel Treybal, Sir George Thomas and Vera Menchik (who put up a decent performance with 7/17). The organizers placed great hopes on the biggest star of Czechoslovakian chess, Salo Flohr, and Flohr indeed took first place with 13 points, half a point ahead of Alekhine.

The leaders performed very consistently – they drew with each other and constantly breathed down each other's necks. Alekhine really wanted to win, but this was not San Remo. Many opponents put up stiff resistance, and even though Alekhine remained undefeated, he made quite a few draws. Before the last round, Flohr's pursuer could still share first place – he only needed to win on demand with white pieces. Alekhine, who drank only cow's milk at the tournament, winning on demand with white? Seems easy enough. But he had to face the stubborn Vladimirs Petrovs.

Game 9
A. Alekhine – V. Petrovs
Podebrady 1936, round 17

Alekhine's play was very energetic, and by the 15th move, the position could have been described with the book cliche "the rest is a matter of technique". However, the Latvian player defended tenaciously and built something akin to a fortress on the board. During the lunch break, the ex-world champion failed to find the strongest plan, missed a queenside jab, started trading pieces and seemingly settled for a draw...

But suddenly, Petrovs started played for a win! A couple of inaccuracies, and the legendary player was unexpectedly pushed to the edge of an abyss.

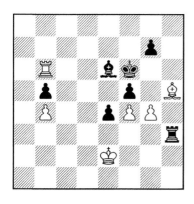

57.♗g6
Since 57.g5+ ♔e7 loses immediately after a check on c4, this move is forced. Alekhine probably thought that transposition to a drawn rook ending was inevitable, but the black king can escape through d8.

57...♔e7! 58.♖b7+
A sad necessity. 58.♗xf5 ♗c4+ 59.♔d1 e3 is pretty bad.

58...♔d8 59.♖b8+ ♔c7 60.♖e8 ♗c4+ 61.♔d2
After 61.♔f2 ♖f3+ 62.♔g2 (62.♔g1 e3 doesn't help) 62...fxg4 63.♖xe4 ♗f1+! 64.♔g1 ♗d3 65.♖e7+ ♔d8 66.♖xg7 ♗xg6 67.♖xg6 ♖xf4, black easily wins. The ex-champion tries another tack, but now the passed g-pawn races for promotion.

61...♖d3+ 62.♔c2 fxg4 63.♖xe4 g3 64.♖e7+
64.♖e5 ♖f3 65.♖g5 ♗f1 doesn't change much.

64...♖d7 65.♖e5 g2 66.♖g5 ♗d5

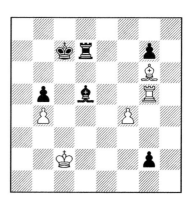

Fantastic! The black pawn is just one step away from the promotion square, and the only thing Petrovs needs to do is to get the rook to help! But this was the 17th round of a very difficult tournament. The game was dragging on, and this time, there was no Euwe to diplomatically offer a draw so that the organizers could hold a closing ceremony. The Latvian master wanted Alekhine's scalp, but the ex-world champion mustered his last strength and managed to create some technical difficulties for white.

67.♔c3 ♗f3 68.♗d3 g6

The iron-fisted 68...♖d8! was the simplest: the rook invades white's camp through the a-file. Instead, Petrovs sacrifices a pawn to break through on the h-file, but Alekhine finds a tactic that hinders this plan.

69.♖xg6 ♖d6 70.♖g7+ ♔b6

71.f5 ♗d5

It turns out that there's no 71...♖h6? 72.♔d2 ♖h1 73.f6 g1=♕? due to 74.♖xg1 ♖xg1 75.f7, and now it's the white pawn that promotes! Petrovs, confused and suffering from time trouble, starts to just move his pieces back and forth, even though the win was still possible!

72.♗e2 ♗c6?

Black easily won with 72...♖d8! 73.♖g6+ ♔c7 74.♗xb5 ♖g8, but it seems that Vladimirs just forgot about the eighth rank...

73.♗d3 ♖d7

Again, 73...♖h6 74.♔d4 ♖h1 75.f6 gives nothing.

74.♖g6 ♖h7?

This was the last chance for black to play 74...♖d6, kick the white rook away, put the bishop on d5 and then the rook on g8. Now, Alekhine happily sacrifices an exchange and captures the g2 pawn – there's a draw on the board!

75.♖xc6+ ♔xc6 76.♗e4+ ♔d6 77.♗xg2 ♖c7+ 78.♔b3 ♖c1

Now 78...♖e7 79.♗f1 ♔c6 80.♗d3 gives nothing: black is tied to the b5 pawn and cannot improve his position.

79.♗e4

Draw. Vladimirs Petrovs fought the formidable Alexander Alekhine on equal terms with the latter already regaining his old form, and if this had not been the last round of a gruelling marathon tournament, he could probably have found the win – it wasn't especially hard.

Despite playing a number of good games, Petrovs finished on an even score – 8.5/17. He finally defeated Steiner, his regular nemesis, drew some games against prizewinners, but lost to a couple of weaker players towards the finish (Skalicka and Pelikan), and this prevented him from taking a higher place.

In 1936, an unofficial chess Olympiad was held in Munich. Germany was not a FIDE member at the time (it had been excluded for the persecution of Jewish chess players), but desperately wanted to hold a big chess event. As a result, the FIDE Congress made a decision: the tournament wasn't considered a true Olympiad, and every country decided on its own whether it wanted to send a team to Nazi Germany. Some leading chess countries refused to take part (including the United States and England), but 22 teams still came to the tournament, even though some were weakened (for instance, Alekhine didn't play for France).

The first board was a bit weaker than in Warsaw, but the line-up was still impressive: Mikenas, Richter, Rejfir, Alexandrescu, Steiner, Stahlberg, Pirc, Eliskases and, of course, Keres!

Petrovs, as usual, was the leading scorer for his team, with 13.5/20. But he couldn't keep up with the Estonian team leader: Paul Keres scored two full points more! The race of the leaders was relentless, but the Latvian made a number of disappointing mistakes that allowed Keres to surge ahead. Petrovs blundered against Pirc, then lost to Romi despite having an overwhelming position, and lost to Richter right out of the opening (the Germans performed well at their home olympiad, taking 3rd place). Still, everything could have turned

out differently, if not for the endgame of their head-to-head encounter.

Game 10
V. Petrovs – P. Keres
Munich 1936, round 8
(Latvia – Estonia)

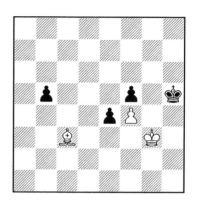

White faced difficulties in the opening, losing a pawn, but Keres carelessly allowed his opponent to retain the bishop pair, and Petrovs put up a good defense. The Estonian tried to squeeze more than was possible from the position and had to give up a piece to stop the passed pawn supported by the two rampaging bishops. And then something strange happened: in this position, Vladimirs accepted a draw! Maybe he thought that if he targeted the f5 pawn, black would have enough time to trade his passed pawn for the bishop? But he actually doesn't: 57.♔f2 ♔g4 (57... ♔g6 58.♔e3 ♔f7 59.♔d4 ♔e6 60.♔c5 is also bad) 58.♔e3 ♔g3 59.♗a5 ♔g4 60.♗e1! ♔h3 61.♔d4 ♔g2 62.♔e5 ♔f1 63.♗b4 e3 64.♔xf5 e2 65.♔e4 e1=♛+ 66.♗xe1 ♔xe1

67.f5 b4 68.♔d4! The white king stops the b5 pawn, the white passed pawn queens, and white wins. He could have at least played some more moves at the board – it's never too late to agree a draw. A mystery, all in all. Still, a +7 score on first board was a great achievement!

Vladimirs Petrovs' successes led to a surge in popularity of chess in Latvia. And then, in 1937, a momentous event happened: the first Latvian supertournament, held at the mud resort of Kemeri!

The line-up of the Kemeri tournament was formidable. Five future AVRO 1938 participants came to Latvia: Alekhine, Keres, Flohr, Fine and Reshevsky! In addition, there were Steiner, Stahlberg, Tartakower, Rellstab, Mikenas and Landau. It was hard for the local players (except for Petrovs, of course) to compete in such a strong tournament, but Apsenieks, even though he finished with a minus score, managed to draw with Flohr, Keres and Alekhine. This gave a micro-advantage to Vladimirs Petrovs – he knew his teammates very well and routinely defeated them all. However, Petrovs' tournament started with a disappointing loss to Reshevsky.

Petrovs outplayed his opponent in good style in a sharp Meran line and was very close to winning. Alas, his games with Reshevsky often followed the same scenario: the Latvian player lost one overwhelming

position after another. Petrovs' American opponent's behavior at the board was not always respectful. In his constant time trouble, the former wonderkid would whack the clock, placed his head on the board to see how much time he still had, thereby impeding his opponent's thought processes, and offered draws in a worse position on every move, sometimes more than once per move. Having said that, Reshevsky's play was immensely strong in time trouble: he calculated short lines very well, easily spotted spectacular tactics and often won games shortly after the first time control. This game was no exception.

Game 11
S. Reshevsky – V. Petrovs
Kemeri 1937, round 1

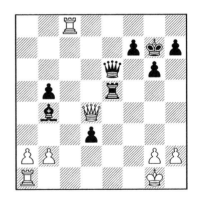

35...♔h6??

Black won with the simple 35...d2 or 35...♕e7, but the most spectacular line was shown by Euwe: 35...♗d2! 36.♔h1 (white gets a hopeless endgame down two pawns

Latvia vs. Estonia, March 1938. The Latvian team won this time, in Reval (today's Tallinn)

after 36.♖c6 ♗e3+ 37.♕xe3 ♖xe3 38.♖xe6 fxe6 39.♖d1 ♔f6 [39...e5 40.♖d2! is too rash] 40.♔f2 ♖e2+ 41.♔f3 ♖xb2 42.♖xd3 ♖xa2 43.♖b3 ♖a5) 36...♗e3 37.♕c3 b4 38.♕c6 ♕xc6 39.♖xc6 ♗c5 40.g3 d2, winning. Unfortunately for Petrovs, he found another "way" to win and blundered a rook. Reshevsky, as usual, had mere seconds on the clock, but...

36.♕xb4 ♕xc8 37.♕f4+! ♖g5 38.h4 ♕c5+ 39.♔h1

Black resigned.

This loss was a huge blow for Vladimirs, and he was unrecognizable in the next two rounds. His opening play against Tartakower was awful, and he only

managed to survive because of his opponent's inaccuracies. Then he failed to convert a big advantage against Ozols, who only scored 3.5/17 in the tournament. The game against Stahlberg in round 4 was a turning point.

Game 12
V. Petrovs – G. Stahlberg
Kemeri 1937, round 4
Queen's Gambit Declined

1.d4 d5 2.c4 c6 3.♘f3 ♘f6 4.♘c3 e6 5.♗g5 h6 6.♗xf6 ♕xf6 7.♕b3 dxc4 8.♕xc4 ♘d7 9.e4 e5 10.d5 ♘b6 11.♕b3 ♗c5 12.♗e2 0-0 13.0-0 ♗g4 14.♖ac1 ♖fd8 15.♘d1 ♗xf3 16.♕xf3 ♕xf3 17.♗xf3

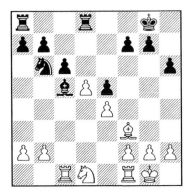

Petrovs' opening play was quite accurate – he tried to avoid risk in the game against a strong opponent. The queens are traded, opposite-colored bishops are on the board, but the position still has some hidden dangers. Here, black could have played 17...♗d4 18.dxc6 ♖ac8 19.c7

♖d7 20.♗g4 ♖dxc7 21.♘c3 ♖d8 22.♘b5, with a drawish position. But Stahlberg, probably taking Petrovs' poor start into account, wants more. He sacrifices a pawn and invades the second rank with his rook.

17...♘d7!? 18.dxc6 bxc6 19.♗g4 ♗b6 20.♖xc6 ♘f6 21.♗f3 ♖d2

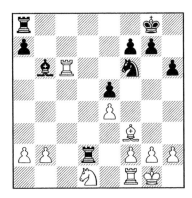

A dramatic loss to Reshevsky. Kemeri, 1937

It seems that white is in trouble. The black bishop is very strong, white's extra pawn isn't particularly noticeable, and the a8 rook can't wait to get to d4. But white shows his composure and pushes his queenside pawns.

22.a4 ♖ad8?

Stahlberg doesn't think that he's in any danger from white's counterplay, and this gets him into trouble. He had to play the precise prophylactic move 22...♖b8!, with equality on the board after 23.b4 ♖d4 24.a5 ♗d8 25.♘e3 ♖dxb4 26.♘c4 ♖4b5.

23.b4 ♖8d4?

The last mistake. After 23...♖a2! 24.a5 ♗d4 25.♘e3 ♗xe3 26.fxe3 ♖b8 27.♖c4! (neither 27.♖b1 ♖xa5 nor 27.♖c5 ♖xb4 28.♖xe5 ♖ba4 29.♖e7 ♔f8! [29...♖xa5 30.e5 loses] 30.♖xa7 ♖xa5 gives white anything), black still has to work for the draw. Now, however, the black bishop gets pushed back to d8, and the white knight joins the fray with a decisive effect.

**24.♖c8+   ♔h7   25.a5   ♗d8
26.♘e3!**

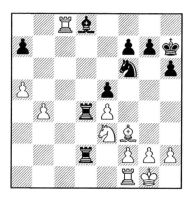

It turns out that capturing either white pawn leads to material losses, but what can black do? In desperation, Stahlberg gave up an exchange, but this led to a quick loss.

**26...♖xb4   27.♘d5   ♖xd5
28.exd5 ♗xa5 29.♖d1 ♖b2 30.♔f1
♗b6 31.♗e2 ♘e4 32.♖c6 ♗d4
33.d6 ♘f6 34.♖c7 ♖b6 35.♖xd4
exd4 36.♗d3+ g6 37.♖xf7+.** Black resigned.

After this win, Petrovs' fortunes changed: he won two more games, against Book and Rellstab. Reshevsky was in the lead with 5.5/6, trailed sensationally by Apsenieks, who had 4.5 points. Petrovs, Flohr, Tartakower and Alekhine had 4 points each, and Fine and Keres didn't enjoy the best of starts – only 3 points. I think that the flying start of Vladimirs' chief Latvian rival affected his subsequent performance in a big way. "How can he overtake me in a supertournament in our home country?" And so, Petrovs surged ahead with lightning speed. Keres barely managed to survive against him, then the Riga player defeated Hasenfuss with black, and then came the day of Fine's reckoning.

Game 13
V. Petrovs – R. Fine
Kemeri 1937, round 9

There's a cliche in chess literature that Petrovs only played closed

openings with white, especially
the Catalan. The Riga player was
a much more versatile player than
that. Of course, he played 1.e4
less often than 1.d4, but if his
opponent had a dangerous non-
classical opening such as Alekhine's
Defense in his repertoire, Vladimirs
considered it a matter of principle
to refute it. He played 1.e2-e4
against both Fine and Flohr, and
his illustrious opponents who met
it with the king's knight move lost
the opening duel with a bang. The
American, however, played rather
inventively and almost managed to
equalize.

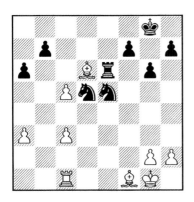

27.♖b1?!
Petrovs launches a tempting
combination, but it turns out to
be flawed. He first had to prevent
the liberating b7-b5 with 27.a4!,
and after 27...♘e3 28.♖b1 ♘5c4
29.♗xc4 ♘xc4 30.♗c7, white has
great chances of success.
  **27...b5! 28.cxb6 ♖xd6 29.b7
♘c6**

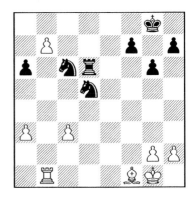

White has sacrificed a piece, but
immediately regaining the piece only
led to a draw. Petrovs is still trying
to find more resources, overstepping
the boundaries of safety.
  30.c4
  30.♖d1 ♖d7 31.♗xa6 ♘f6
32.♖xd7 ♘xd7 33.♗b5 ♘db8 was
bad: the black king is in time to stop
the white pawns.
  30...♘e3 31.♖b6?
  31.c5 ♖d2 (31...♖d1 32.♖xd1
♘xd1 33.♗xa6 ♘c3 34.a4 ♔f8
35.♗b5 ♘b8 36.c6 ♘d5 37.a5
♘c7 38.a6 ♘cxa6 39.♗xa6 ♘xc6
40.♔f2 ♔e7 41.♗c4 loses) 32.♖e1
(after 32.♖b6 ♘b8 33.c6 ♖c2, black
eliminates the white pawns) 32...♘f5
led to nothing more than equality.
Petrovs pours more gasoline onto
the fire, but at first Fine finds the
correct replies.
  **31...♖d1!   32.♔f2   ♖xf1+!
33.♔xe3 ♘b8**
  Out of many moves and lines,
Reuben Fine finds the only way
– not just to a draw, but to an
advantage! It turns out that despite
the passive positions of the black

Kemeri tournament participants in the dunes of Jurmala. July 1937

king and knight, white cannot land a decisive blow!

34.♖d6 ♖e1+ 35.♔d4

The alternative, 35.♔d2, also led to a joyless rook endgame: 35...♖e8 36.c5 ♔g7 37.c6 ♖e7 38.♔c3 ♖c7 39.♔d4 ♘xc6+ 40.♖xc6 ♖xb7; the a6 pawn falls, but the black rook gets to the second rank.

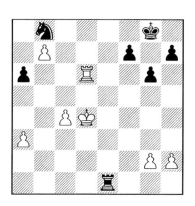

Now, 35...♔g7! would have forced white to scramble for a draw in a difficult rook ending: 36.c5 ♖b1 37.c6 ♘xc6, transposing into the line above, but Fine, tired of the complicated fight, decided to send his king closer to the pawns and misses a pretty rook maneuver in time trouble.

35...♔f8? 36.♖d8+ ♖e8 37.♖c8!

White wins an important tempo and can now get his king to d6!

37...♔e7 38.♔d5 ♖d8+ 39.♖xd8 ♔xd8 40.♔d6

Black resigned, since the white pawns are unstoppable. Petrovs' tenacity paid off after all!

Afterwards, Vladimirs defeated Bergs, drew with Steiner, and in round 12 he won the derby duel against Apsenieks, who was already slowly drifting towards the lower half of the table. Meanwhile, Reshevsky lost to Alekhine, but still led with 10/12. Petrovs jumped to second place with 9 points. He was trailed by Flohr (8.5), Keres, Alekhine (both 8), Steiner, Tartakower (both 7), Mikenas, Fine, Apsenieks (all 6.5), and Stahlberg (6).

Petrovs' next opponent was Alexander Alekhine. It was the ex-world champion's last big tournament before his return match against Euwe. In the previous rounds, Alekhine had lost to Mikenas and made some unnecessary draws, including one with Book. To uphold his reputation and continue his fight for first place he desperately needed to defeat the Latvian, but Petrovs played very accurately and made a draw with white. Alekhine fought like a lion, but couldn't get anything more than a drawn bishop ending with an extra pawn.

Petrovs withstood the onslaught of his most dangerous opponent, but the game against Mikenas in the next round proved to be much more difficult.

Game 14
V. Mikenas – V. Petrovs
Kemeri 1937, round 14
Queen's Gambit Declined

Vladas Mikenas was a long-time leader of the Lithuanian chess players. He had an immense tactical talent and posed a danger to any strong master or grandmaster – for instance, he had an equal score against Alekhine. Later, Vladas Ionovich became a prominent arbiter and refereed one of the matches between Karpov and Kasparov. The top three players of Baltic chess (Keres, Petrovs and Mikenas) were friends, but their games were generally sharp and usually didn't end in draws.

1.d4 d5 2.c4 e6 3.♘c3 ♘f6 4.♗g5 ♗e7 5.e3 ♘bd7 6.♘f3 0-0 7.♖c1 a6 8.a3 dxc4 9.♗xc4 b5 10.♗a2 c5 11.0-0 ♗b7 12.♗b1 ♛b6 13.♘e5 ♖fd8

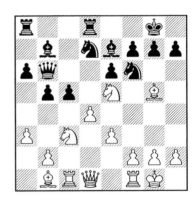

Petrovs has played the opening in a classical way and solved the problem of his light-squared bishop, but his eagle-eyed opponent finds a way to create a small storm on the chess board.

14.♘xd7! ♖xd7 15.♗xf6 ♗xf6?
Petrovs liked bishop pairs (and other kinds of static advantages), so

he was even ready to give up a pawn for that, but 15...gxf6! was stronger: 16.dxc5 (the lunge 16.♕g4+ ♔h8 17.♕h5 f5 18.♕xf7 cxd4 gives nothing) 16...♖xd1 17.cxb6 ♖xc1! 18.♖xc1 ♖c8 with equality, and if 19.♖d1 then 19...♗xa3.

16.dxc5?!

Strictly speaking, 16.♕h5 g6 17.♕xc5 ♕xc5 18.dxc5 was stronger. But Mikenas didn't start all that to settle for a boring endgame...

16...♕c6 17.♕g4 ♕xc5

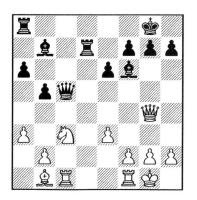

18.♘a4!?

A cunning move! Another possibility was 18.♘e4 ♕e7 19.♘c5 ♗xb2 20.♖c2 ♗xa3 (20... ♖c7 21.♘xb7 ♖xc2 22.♗xc2 ♖c8 23.♕e4 f5 24.♕d3 ♕xb7 25.♕b3 loses) 21.♘xd7 ♕xd7 22.♖d1 ♕e7 23.♖cd2 ♗c6: with a complicated position where black has good compensation for the exchange. Instead, Mikenas sets a nasty trap. After 18.♘a4, black still can play 18...♕e7 19.♘b6 and take on b2, getting a position similar to the line above. But he can also retreat

to a7 without sacrificing anything, right? Wrong! He walks right into the trap.

18...♕a7? 19.♘c5 ♖c7

19...♖e7 20.♘xb7 ♖xb7 21.♗e4 ♗xb2 22.♕f3 loses. Petrovs thought that he could save the exchange because of the weakness of the first rank, but he missed a crafty blow.

20.♘xe6!

Black was counting on 20.♘xb7 ♖xc1 21.♖xc1 ♕xb7 22.♗e4 ♖c8 with equality.

20...♖xc1 21.♖xc1 ♕b6

It turns out that after 21...fxe6 22.♕xe6+ ♔h8 23.♕f5 ♔g8 24.♖c7 white delivers checkmate. Black is forced to give up a pawn, and after **22.♘g5**, Mikenas scored a brilliant and energetic win.

I should point out that Petrovs would often play hesitantly if his opponent tried to checkmate him right out of the opening. This trait showed up most clearly in his games against Keres (and Eliskases), and Vladimirs would tell his wife that he was afraid of Paul...

Petrovs was pushed back to third place with 9.5 points, behind Reshevsky (10.5/14, he lost to Rellstab) and Flohr (10/14). The Czech player was in his element: he obliterated the tail-enders and drew versus all the stronger opposition. Petrovs was trailed by Alekhine and Keres (9 each), Steiner (8.5), and Tartakower (8). Fine shared 8th place with Mikenas and Apsenieks (7.5/14).

In round 15, Petrovs skillfully outplayed Landau in the endgame, and Flohr drew with Stahlberg, so they both were one point behind Reshevsky, with Keres and Alekhine in hot pursuit. In round 16, Reshevsky could have lost his leadership: the American got into a difficult position against Stahlberg and only escaped thanks to a miracle. Petrovs and Flohr won again, and the situation before the last round became incredibly tense: 1. Reshevsky – 12/16, 2–3. Flohr, Petrovs – 11.5; 4–5. Keres, Alekhine – 11. The leader had black against the Finnish master Book, Alekhine had black against Bergs,

Keres had white against Feigins, and Petrovs and Flohr faced each other.

All potential winners had to tackle their nerves. Both Alekhine and Keres played terribly in the opening and could easily have resigned as early as on the 25th move! Reshevsky committed to playing for a win with black and selected the Alekhine's Defense (which was extensively deployed in the tournament – it was quite fashionable at the time! Alekhine's daring idea won the hearts of the leading chess players). The Finnish master didn't perform too well in the tournament, but managed to pull himself together in the last round and created a powerful initiative – it

Another win against Landau. Kemeri, round 15, 1937

became clear that Reshevsky would soon lose material. So Petrovs now had an incredible chance to win the immensely strong tournament outright! Here is the true decisive "battle of Kemeri"!

Game 15
V. Petrovs – S. Flohr
Kemeri 1937, round 17
Alekhine's Defense

1.e4 ♘f6 2.e5 ♘d5 3.d4 d6 4.c4 ♘b6 5.exd6 exd6 6.♘c3 ♘c6 7.♗e3 ♗e7 8.♗d3 0-0 9.♘ge2 ♗g4 10.0-0 ♖e8 11.h3 ♗h5 12.♕d2 ♗g6 13.♗xg6 hxg6 14.b3 ♗f8 15.d5 ♘e7 16.♗g5 ♕d7 17.♘d4 c5 18.♘f3 ♘f5

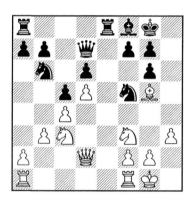

It may be hard to believe, but Flohr, who usually plays defensively, also tried to play for a win here. Instead of the usual Caro-Kann, he played the Alekhine's Defense, probably thinking that Petrovs would go for the sharp Four Pawns Attack that he played against Fine. However, Vladimirs was

well-prepared, played 5.exd6 this time, and soon the Czechoslovak grandmaster was on the ropes. Black's position is gloomy. One of his knights is entombed on the queenside, the other one will soon be kicked from f5, and the f8 bishop is restricted by its own pawns. Even if Flohr manages to trade all rooks, this won't make it easier for him: black's woes are serious and long-term.

19.♖ae1 a6

19...f6 20.♗f4 g5 21.♗h2 ♖xe1 22.♖xe1 ♖e8 23.♘e4 doesn't improve the situation: white has a couple more pieces in play, the said pieces are targeting the d6 square, and there's a threat g2-g4. Flohr makes the only possible decision in this position: he provokes white to push the g-pawn immediately to try and force simplifications on the kingside.

20.g4

White could improve his position with 20.♘e4, but can we really say that a move that forces the knight to retreat to the edge of the board is bad?

20...♘h6

Of course, not 20...♘e7 21.♗f4 ♖ad8 22.♘e4 ♘ec8, and now both knights are stuck on the queenside.

21.♕f4 f5!?

Black can't trade rooks: after 21...♖xe1 22.♖xe1 ♖e8 23.♖xe8 ♕xe8 24.♘e4, white threatens both d6 and h6. Now white has a concrete task ahead of him.

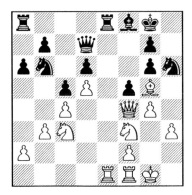

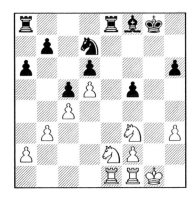

22.♗xh6!?

Petrovs sees an opportunity to go for a favorable endgame. But white already has more pieces in play, and it's enough to consolidate forces for the decisive attack: 22.♘h4! ♚h7 (the king move is the most tenacious; 22...fxg4 23.♘e4 ♘f7 24.hxg4 ♘e5 25.♕g3 ♕xg4 26.♕xg4 ♘xg4 27.♘xg6 ♘e5 28.♘xe5 dxe5 [28...♖xe5 29.♗f4] 29.♖e3 leads to a lost endgame, while after 22...♖xe1, there's 23.♖xe1 ♖e8 24.♖xe8 ♕xe8 25.gxf5 ♘xf5 [25...♕e1+ 26.♔g2 ♕xc3 27.fxg6 ♘d7 28.♗xh6 doesn't help] 26.♘e4 with a huge advantage) 23.♔h2 fxg4 24.♘e4, with strong threats. Still, Petrovs' decision doesn't throw away the win just yet.

22...gxh6 23.gxf5 ♕xf5 24.♕xf5

24.♕g3! ♔g7 25.♘h4 ♕g5 26.♕xg5 hxg5 27.♘f3 ♔h6 28.♔h2 was more precise; this endgame is fairly easily won for white.

24...gxf5 25.♘e2 ♘d7

25...♖e4 26.♘g3 ♖f4 27.♖e3 ♔f7 28.♖fe1 a5 29.♘h5 loses either a pawn or an exchange.

26.♘f4?

The main mystery of this game. Why didn't white just take the pawn? – 26.♘g3 f4 27.♘h5. Now Flohr activates his minor pieces and can harbor some hopes to save the game.

26...♗g7 27.♘e6?!

It was better to play 27.♘h4 ♖e4 28.♖xe4 fxe4 29.♘e6 ♗e5 30.♖e1 ♘f6 31.f4 exf3 32.♔f2: the second white knight gets to f5, keeping up the steady pressure. Now black takes the h4 square under control and equalizes.

27...♗f6! 28.♔h2 ♔f7 29.♔g3 ♗e5+! 30.♘xe5+ ♘xe5 31.f4 ♘d7

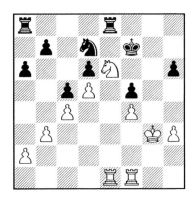

Flohr has again shown his brilliant defensive skills and has saved a completely hopeless position! Petrovs probably thought that the Czechoslovak grandmaster would now force the trade of the last pair of minor pieces through f8, but he failed to anticipate his opponent's idea. The e6 knight is not dangerous now – Flohr can just work around it and put his own knight on e4.

32.♔h4?!

32.♔f3 ♘f6 33.♖g1 ♖g8 led to equality. Petrovs wanted to trade on f8 and then go forward with his king, but...

32...♘f6! 33.♖g1 ♖g8 34.♖g3? ♖xg3 35.♔xg3 ♖g8+ 36.♔h2 ♘e4

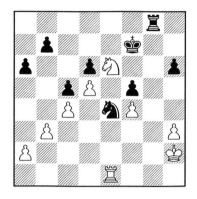

Black's position is already better. The white knight is out of play, and Flohr can play the break b7-b5 now. The correct continuation for white was of course to put the rook on e2 and then play a4, but this still wouldn't have solved all the problems. And so Petrovs makes a mistake that... saves the game.

37.♖g1? ♖xg1 38.♔xg1 ♔e7?

Before time control, Flohr didn't dare to play the sharp 38...b5!, but black had just enough tempi to weaken the white pawn chain and stop the a-pawn from moving: 39.♘c7 (39.cxb5 axb5 40.a4 c4 is bad as well) 39...bxc4 40.bxc4 ♘d2 41.♘xa6 ♘xc4 42.♘c7 ♘b6, retaining some chances of success in a sharp knight endgame – the king goes to d7. Now white slips out of it!

39.♔g2 ♘c3 40.♘g7! ♔f6

40...♘xa2 41.♘xf5+ ♔d7 42.♘xh6 ♘c1 43.h4 ♘xb3 44.♘f5 is too risky for black, so Flohr wisely decided to repeat moves.

41.♘e8+ ♔e7. Draw!

In 1937, a long time ago. After a three-week battle in Kemeri

The final round, a decisive battle with Flohr. Kemeri, 4 July 1937

Alekhine and Keres managed to save their games; however, Book was implacable and precise – Reshevsky fought until the bitter end, but ultimately resigned. As a result, Flohr, Petrovs and Reshevsky shared first place with 12 points. Vladimirs Petrovs lost an incredible opportunity. Had he won that last game, he would have taken outright first place, defeating the grandmaster who was handpicked by Alekhine for a potential world championship match! Without a doubt, after such a success, Petrovs would have been invited to the AVRO tournament. But, alas...

Still, it was an incredible success for Latvian chess. A local player competed on equal terms with the greatest chess luminaries. Vladimirs Petrovs' brilliant result delighted the chess world, his name regularly appeared in the press – and since 1937, it referred to him as "Grandmaster Vladimirs Petrovs"!

On an Equal Footing with Alekhine and Capablanca

Riga applauded loudly! Overtaking Alexander Alekhine himself and sharing first place with the titans of modern chess who were designated as future world champion candidates by the press was no mean feat. Newspapers and magazines published headline articles about the Latvian player's success in Kemeri, and the new grandmaster basked in the rays of glory. Petrovs quickly received an invitation to one of the strongest tournaments of the pre-war era – the double round-robin 8-player tournament in Semmering. The same format was used in the AVRO tournament.

In addition to the Rigan, the field included such stars as Reshevsky, Flohr, Keres, Fine and even Capablanca! The organizers wanted to invite the leader of Soviet chess as well, but Botvinnik and Levenfish were preparing for their Soviet Championship match, and so they settled for Vyacheslav Ragozin, Botvinnik's long-term second and coach. The strongest Austrian grandmaster, Erich Eliskases, was the eighth participant. Since Euwe and Alekhine were set to face each other in the return match that autumn, all the strongest players in the world, except for the participants of those Soviet and Dutch matches, were due to gather in Semmering. Petrovs was looking forward to the new tournament. He'd never faced Capablanca before and couldn't wait for a chance to sit at the board with the great Cuban. Only two months remained until Semmering; who could have thought that Vladimirs Petrovs would now experience one of the most difficult periods of his career?

Meanwhile, the Stockholm Olympiad was scheduled for July 1937, and Latvia was all excited before the upcoming Tournament of Nations. The authors of numerous articles in the press set incredible targets for the Baltic team – up to and including a top-3 finish! Of course they could do that – they now had a mighty leader, a player known and respected all around the world. Even though the travel budget was modest, as always, Petrovs was allowed to take his wife with him to Sweden – conditions for the first-board player had to be as comfortable as possible. However, shortly before the start, the Latvian team suffered a heavy loss: Master Feigins, who performed extremely well in Folkestone and Munich, winning a board medal at both competitions, declined to travel to Sweden. The severely weakened team had to play all 19 rounds almost without substitutions. But even that was not all: the Swedish organizers tried a dubious experiment. To cut costs, they decided to hold two rounds per day with an exotic time control (proposed at the FIDE Congress in Warsaw): 2.5 hours per 50 moves. 11 hours of play per day! Still, despite all the hardships, Vladimirs Petrovs' team arrived at the Grand Hotel Royal and prepared for battle. They were drawn to face the Netherlands in round 1, then they had a bye in round 2 and were scheduled to play Estonia in round 3.

The Dutch team was led by the world champion Max Euwe. The future FIDE president had to defend his title in the upcoming return match against Alekhine, but, despite the incredibly difficult time control and the unthinkable two-rounds-per-day schedule, Euwe decided to go to Stockholm (Alekhine refused to play at the Olympiad, which essentially led to the withdrawal of the French team). Max the Fifth was not only a gentleman through and through, but a hero of his homeland. Thus, Petrovs had to face Euwe first, and then, after a short rest, he had Keres the next day. A difficult, but very interesting start – especially considering that the Latvian grandmaster had never faced a reigning world champion before. The Dutchman was considered an expert on the 4.♕c2 line of the Nimzo-Indian for both colors (however, in the world championship return match, he suffered two heavy defeats in the opening duel precisely in this line – and after two brilliant wins in games 8 and 10, Alekhine irrevocably

seized the initiative in the match). Several years before Stockholm, Euwe got a surefire advantage with white against Capablanca: after 1.d4 ♘f6 2.c4 e6 3.♘c3 ♗b4 4.♕c2 d5 5.a3 ♗xc3+ 6.♕xc3 dxc4 7.♕xc4 0–0 8.♗g5, the ex-world champion played the passive 8...c6, got a dismal position and escaped by the skin of his teeth (Short's recipe, 7...b6 or 8...b6, intending to develop the light-squared bishop to a6, would only become known in 1998 – can you imagine?). Later, however, Lisitsin, Ragozin and Kan tested the aggressive line 6...♘e4 7.♕c2 c5!? in several Soviet tournaments: white should either settle for full equality or take the c5 pawn, getting behind in development and facing a dangerous position. This line became fashionable in modern times, but back then, it was a revelation, and Vladimirs Petrovs knew the idea well. All in all, the leader of the Latvian team was well-prepared for his battle with the champion, but... According to Petrovs' wife, Vladimirs Mikhailovich decided to quit smoking the day before and suffered severe withdrawal symptoms during the night. The symptoms became milder in the morning, but didn't end completely: Petrovs was pale and nauseous. And several hours later, the grandmaster had to face the world champion at the board. The latter confidently pushed his queen's pawn two squares forward.

Game 16
M. Euwe – V. Petrovs
Stockholm 1937, round 1
(Netherlands – Latvia)
Nimzo-Indian Defense

1.d4 ♘f6 2.c4 e6 3.♘c3 ♗b4 4.♕c2 d5 5.a3 ♗xc3+ 6.♕xc3 ♘e4 7.♕c2 c5 8.dxc5 ♘c6

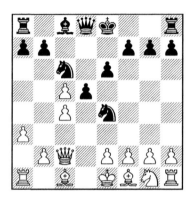

It's too dangerous to go for the most principled line, 9.cxd5 exd5 10.♘f3 ♗f5 11.b4, without preparation; also, such pawn-grabbing was considered bad taste back then. So, white preferred the modest **9.e3 ♕a5+ 10.♗d2 ♘xd2 11.♕xd2 dxc4! 12.♗xc4 ♕xc5**, and black managed to completely equalize.

13.♖c1 ♕g5 14.f4 ♕h4+ 15.♕f2 ♕xf2+ 16.♔xf2 ♔e7 17.♘f3 ♖d8 18.♗b5 ♗d7 19.♖c3 a6 20.♗a4 b5 21.♗b3 ♖ac8 22.♖hc1 ♘a5 23.♗a2 ♖xc3 24.♖xc3 ♖c8 25.♖xc8 ♗xc8

So, both queens and rooks were off the board...

It seems that the position is completely equal – how can anyone

win here? However, it's not that simple: the a6 and b5 pawns are fixed on the squares of the same color as the black bishop, and so Petrovs still had to be careful. It's white to move, and Euwe sets a cunning positional trap for his opponent.

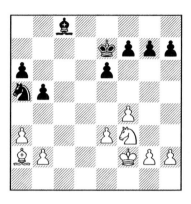

26.♘d4!

And now it suddenly turns out that the natural-looking 26...♗b7 is not the best move. After 27.b4!, black faces an unpleasant choice: either 27...♘c6 28.♘b3, completely ceding the c5 square to the opponent, or allow him to disconnect the pawns, relying on the bishop's strength against the knight with 27...♘c4 28.♗xc4 bxc4 29.g3. For instance, after 29...♗e4?! 30.♔e2 ♔d6 (30...c3 31.♔d1 ♔d6 32.♘b3! ♔d5 33.♘c5 is bad as well) 31.♔d2 f6 32.♘e2, black is faced with an unpleasant defense. It's better to bring the king to e4 with the subsequent idea h5-h4; black can probably save the game, but the risk is big enough, so there's really no point in pursuing this route. In reply, black withdraws the knight from a tempo attack and relocates it to c5 to put pressure on the important e4 square.

26...♞b7 27.e4 ♞c5 28.♔e3 ♝b7 29.♝b1 f6

To hold the center, white had to retreat his bishop to b1, and now black only has to play e6-e5, putting a barrier before the white king. Euwe has nothing else to do than harass the black knight.

30.b4

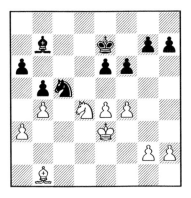

"Chess is a very simple game. You only have to make correct choices between active and prophylactic moves," David Bronstein used to say. Ah, such choices can be so incredibly hard sometimes! Indeed, where should the black knight go? Paradoxically, the retreat to f8 allowed black to easily hold the position: 30...♞d7 31.♝a2 ♞f8 32.g3 ♔d6 — the g2 pawn is weak, so white has no time to play e4-e5, and Petrovs only had to cover the f5 square and play e6-e5 with a draw. Alas, the pseudo-active move to a4 turns out to be a poor choice.

30...♞a4?! 31.♝c2! ♞b6

Of course, 31...♞c3 32.♞b3 ♞a4 33.♞a5 is bad, but perhaps black had been counting on 31...♔d6 32.♝xa4 bxa4. At first glance, it seems that the weakness of the a4 pawn is insignificant, and it's hard for white to restructure his position, but Euwe would have most probably found the pretty resource 33.♞f3!: now white threatens to invade with the king, and 33...e5 is met with 34.fxe5+ fxe5 35.♞g5! h6 36.♞f7+, and, due to the threat of a fork on d8, the white knight snatches a pawn! So, the knight has to retreat, and this means that black just gifted some tempi to his opponent.

32.♝b3 ♝c8?!

Discouraged by such a sudden change in fortunes, black failed to find the only move 32...e5! 33.♞f5+ (33.♞e6 exf4+ 34.♔xf4 g5+ gives nothing) 33...♔f8 34.fxe5 fxe5 35.♞d6 ♝a8 36.♞f7 ♞d7; incredibly, white has no decisive moves. Now, however, the world champion puts his own pawn on that square, fixing a third black pawn on a light square.

33.e5 fxe5 34.fxe5

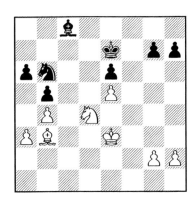

34...♗b7?

Vladimirs Petrovs doesn't want to settle for passive defense, so he gives up a pawn to trade off his "bad" bishop and try to save the game with as little material left as possible. After 34...♗d7, white would start an attack with the g- and h-pawns, creating a new weakness there, which, coupled with the unprotected c5 square and opportunities for his king breaking through, would have given Euwe good winning chances. Petrovs probably didn't believe that he could defend that position. But after the game move, he loses by force.

35.♘xe6 ♗d5 36.♘c5 ♗xb3 37.♘xb3 ♘c4+ 38.♔e4 ♘xa3 39.♘c5 ♘c2 40.♘xa6 ♔d7

Now white has a healthy extra pawn in a knight endgame and a won position.

41.♔d5?!

A serious inaccuracy. The opponents were already in time trouble (time control was only on move 50!). The Dutchman was in too much of a hurry to create an outside passed pawn and could have made his task much more difficult. After the simple 41.♘c5+ ♔e7 42.♘d3 ♔e6, white only had to put his opponent in zugzwang and take the b5 pawn in much more favorable conditions.

41...♘e3+   42.♔c5   ♔e6 43.♔xb5

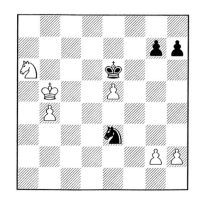

43...♔xe5?

Black takes the wrong pawn, missing the sudden opportunity. Of course, the e5 pawn wasn't going anywhere, so he had to take on g2 and then try to sacrifice his knight for the white passed pawn: 43...♘xg2! Euwe would have needed to demonstrate some study-like technique to win: 44.♔c5! (44.♔c6 ♔xe5 45.b5 ♘e3 46.b6 ♘c4 leads to a draw – black easily gets rid of the last white pawn) 44...♘e1 45.b5 (45.♔c6 ♘c2 gives nothing) 45...♘d3+ 46.♔d4! ♘xe5 47.♘c7+ ♔d6 (after 47...♔f5 48.b6 ♘c6+, white pushes the black knight aside in a very instructive way and queens his pawn: 49.♔d5 ♘d8 50.♘b5 h5 51.♘d4+ ♔f6 52.♔d6 ♘b7+ 53.♔c6 ♘a5+ 54.♔c7 g5 55.♘c6 ♘b3 56.♔d6!) 48.♘e8+ ♔e6 (the pawn ending after 48...♔d7 49.♔xe5 ♔xe8 50.♔e6 is lost) 49.♘xg7+ ♔d6 50.♘e8+! ♔e6 51.♔c5, and white should convert his advantage thanks to the presence of the h-pawns.

And white had to find all that in time trouble. However, Petrovs thought that Euwe would play

Stockholm Chess Olympiad: Petrovs vs. Euwe. August 1937

44.♔c6, and after 44...♘xg2 45.b5 ♘e3 46.b6 ♘c4, there would be a draw. He miscalculated, however.

44.♔c5! ♘d5

Alas, now 44...♘xg2 doesn't help black: 45.b5 ♘f4 46.b6 ♘e6+ 47.♔c6 ♘d8+ 48.♔c7 ♘e6+ 49.♔c8 ♘d4 50.b7 ♘c6 51.♘b4, curtains.

45.b5 ♘c3 46.♘c7 ♔e4

Hoping against hope for 47.b6 ♘a4+ 48.♔b5 ♘xb6 49.♔xb6 ♔e3, but white has a stronger reply.

47.♔d6! ♘xb5+ 48.♘xb5 ♔e3 49.♔e5 ♔f2 50.g4

The time control was reached, and Petrovs resigned. Black can capture the h2 pawn, but he won't be able to trade the other pawn. The Latvian team lost 1–3 overall.

Luckily for the Riga player, his team had a bye in the second round,

and it allowed him to recover from his illness. And then an unexpected thing happened: for the only time in history, Keres declined to play against Petrovs! Was it a goodwill gesture from his "friend Paul"? We'll probably never learn the truth now... Another Paul took first board against Latvia – Master Paul Schmidt. The game ended in a quick draw, and Estonia won 2.5–1.5. In the subsequent rounds, Vladimirs Petrovs still did everything he could to conserve his strength – it was hard for him even to stay in the tournament hall, let alone play... His games against Thomas, Castaldi and Gilfer also ended in draws.

In round 7, Latvia faced Scotland, who eventually finished last, and Latvia won 4–0; Petrovs defeated Montgomerie in just 20 moves. And after draws against Mikenas and

Lundin, he finally reached a plus score, bringing victory for his team in the match against Norway.

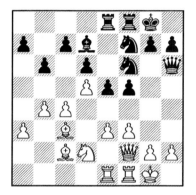

A typical situation for the Nimzo-Indian Defense: white has the bishop pair, but the position is closed, so it's difficult to use the long-range pieces. On the other hand, the Norwegian player has a clear plan for queenside play, but what should black do? His e- and f-pawns need to continue to close the diagonals for his opponent's bishop artillery, while his knights have no outposts. And so, Petrovs made an absolutely correct decision that befuddled his opponent.

23...g5!

It turns out that black is ready to launch a pawn onslaught at the kingside: ♘h8, ♘g6, ♕g7, h5-h4, g4. Of course, the Norwegian player has to counter this by harassing his opponent on the other flank –

24.a4 ♘h8 25.a5 ♘g6 26.axb6 axb6 27.♖a1, with the rook going to a7, but here Herseth, whose play had been decent up until now, panicked and tried to build a defensive wall. Which was only solid at first glance.

24.♖e2 ♘h8 25.e4? f4

Now black's attack continues unhindered, and Petrovs will also essentially have an extra piece in his attack, because the dark-squared bishop cannot help its army.

26.g4 ♘g6 27.♕g2 ♘h4 28.♕h1 ♕g6 29.h3 h5 30.♔f2 ♔f7 31.♔e1 ♖h8 32.♖h2 ♖h6

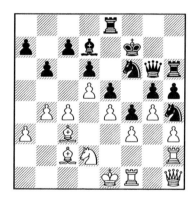

And now it turns out that as soon as the black e-rook gets to h8, a blow on g4 becomes inevitable. Piece sacrifices to gain connected passed pawns often work even if the opponent's pieces are well-positioned, but here, even the white queen is stuck at h1.

33.♔d1 ♖eh8 34.♖ff2

Allowing black to fork the rooks, but, to be fair, white still lost even after both 34.♔c1 ♘xf3! 35.gxh5 (35.♘xf3 hxg4 36.hxg4 ♖xh2

37.♘xh2 ♘xg4) 35...♖xh5 36.♘xf3 ♗xh3 37.♖g1 ♘g4 and 34.♕g1 ♘xf3! 35.♘xf3 hxg4 36.hxg4 ♗xg4 – the pin is decisive here. Now it's all simpler, and all the pretty lines remain behind the scenes.

34...hxg4 35.hxg4 ♗xg4

The piece cannot be taken because of huge material losses, and white resigned after move 46, though he could have resigned right now with a clear conscience.

The next two rounds were truly disappointing for Latvia. Petrovs' team lost 1–3 to Yugoslavia (Petrovs drew with Pirc on board 1) and then to Hungary with the same score; their leader lost to Lilienthal right out of the opening. The formidable Andor had been living in the USSR for two years by then, but still played for his home country and managed to lead the Hungarians to silver medals. All in all, Latvia lost six matches, won four and drew one, falling to the bottom of the table. And they hadn't even played the leaders yet, the United States and Poland! The upcoming matches against the strong Czechoslovakia and Argentina teams didn't exactly inspire optimism either.

However, this moment was a turning point for Latvia, and they performed very well in the second half of the competition. Petrovs saved the match against Argentina by beating Piazzini. The battle against the USA also ended in a 2–2 draw: Reshevsky couldn't do anything

with white against his well-prepared opponent.

The match against mid-table rivals Finland was quite nerve-wracking.

Game 18
V. Petrovs – T. Gauffin
Stockholm 1937, round 15
(Latvia – Finland)

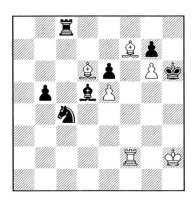

The endgame was played in mutual time trouble. The Finnish team had every reason to hope for Thorsten Gauffin's success: black has an extra pawn, and in the line 45.♔g3 ♘xd6 46.exd6 ♔g5 47.♖b2 ♖d8 48.♖xb5 ♔f6, the "passer in reserve" on g6 should fall soon. White should retain his dark-squared bishop at any price – even if he needs to give up a pawn for that.

45.♗b4!

Petrovs is trying to mount an attack on the enemy king with limited forces. It's rather hard to calculate all the consequences of taking on e5 when your flag is hanging, and Gauffin makes a serious inaccuracy.

45...♔g5?!

It was absolutely necessary to capture the pawn, 45...♘xe5, but after 46.♔g3, it's hard to find the subtle 46...♔h5! (46...♔g5 47.♗d2+ leads to mate). Incredibly, white is unable to weave a mating net! He has to scramble for a draw: 47.♖e2 ♘f3 (47...♘g4 48.♗xe6 ♗xe6 49.♖xe6 immediately leads to a draw) 48.♖xe6! (not 48.♗xe6 ♗xe6 49.♖xe6 ♘d4 50.♖b6 ♖c6 51.♖b7 ♖xg6+, and black again has two extra pawns) 48...♗xe6 49.♗xe6 ♖c6 50.♗g4+ ♔xg6 51.♗xf3 ♖c4, and the bishop pair should save white, even though he would still need to make some precise moves. The king's position on g5, however, is poor – it's exposed to attacks from all of white's pieces. The position sharpens significantly, and white can also try and play for a win now!

46.♔g3

After the only move 46...♖c7 47.♖e2 ♔f5 48.♖f2+ ♔e4 black escapes, but Gauffin got confused and blundered a mate in two.

46...♖a8?? 47.♗e7+ (attacking from the other direction!) **47...♔h5 48.♖h2#**, and Latvia won the match 3–1.

The last few games gave some hope that Petrovs' condition had improved, and that he would show all his strength at the finish, but immediately after that, he lost to Dunkelblum of Belgium. Still, Vladimirs and his teammates performed rather well in the last three matches: the Latvians drew with Czechoslovakia (Petrovs – Flohr was a draw) and deprived Poland of silver medals, defeating the mighty opponents 2.5–1.5 (Tartakower – Petrovs was another draw). In the last round, they brought down Denmark 3–1, with Vladimirs Petrovs defeating Enevoldsen. Latvia finished 11th in the overall table, and Petrovs, who played without being rested, scored +2 – still much lower than that of Reshevsky, Lilienthal, Flohr, Keres, Euwe...

However, the Riga player had much graver concerns than tournament scores: immediately after coming home, he was hospitalized because he still felt sick. The doctor X-rayed him, and the results were shocking: it turned out that the grandmaster had tuberculosis! Vladimirs Petrovs spent a full month in hospital recuperating. And the coveted tournament in Austria was getting closer and closer...

Thankfully, Petrovs got a bit lucky: the Semmering organizers faced some financial trouble, and the event was moved from 25th August to 8th September, with games from round five being played in Baden bei Wien, which allowed the grandmaster to finish his treatment. And so, ultimately, Vladimirs Petrovs did get to take part in his dream tournament.

The first-round pairings were as follows: Capablanca – Fine, Eliskases – Ragozin, Flohr – Keres, and Reshevsky – Petrovs. Vladimirs had to face an uncomfortable opponent – the strongest American grandmaster. The former wonderkid never studied theory and couldn't equalize in the opening against Petrovs – neither with white nor with black. However, as we mentioned earlier, Reshevsky was a brilliant defender, and he often managed to outwit his opponents in the inevitable time trouble. Unfortunately, the same thing happened in this game: Petrovs failed to defeat his slippery opponent, despite having every reason to hope for a win...

Game 19
S. Reshevsky – V. Petrovs
Semmering-Baden 1937, round 1
Queen's Gambit Accepted

1.♘f3 ♘f6 2.d4 d5 3.c4 dxc4 4.e3 e6 5.♗xc4 c5 6.0-0 a6 7.a3 b5 8.♗a2 ♗b7 9.♕e2 ♘bd7 10.♖d1 cxd4 11.♘xd4 ♕b6 12.♘c3 ♗c5 13.♘f3 ♕c6 14.♗d2 ♘e5

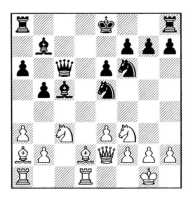

White has handled a well-known tabiya of the Queen's Gambit Accepted quite poorly, and the

Latvian grandmaster has got literally everything he could dream of: space, active pieces, and a battery along the a8-h1 diagonal. Reshevsky had to defend the f3 knight somehow. He could have set a small trap with 15.e4. In this case, the naive 15...♘eg4 is met with the devastating 16.♗d5! But, of course, the American didn't like the simple 15...♘xf3+ 16.gxf3 0–0 – white has no compensation for his weakened kingside. And so, white had no qualms about retreating to the first rank with his knight. We should point out that such "pirouettes" occurred rather often in Samuel Reshevsky's games: the grandmaster would frequently get unpleasant positions with white and tried to extinguish his opponent's initiative without weakening his own position. And to do that, one needs to engage in trench warfare.

15.♘e1 ♖d8 16.f3 0–0 17.♔h1

A useful prophylactic move. After 17.♖ac1 ♕b6, white had to play 18.b4 (18.♔h1 ♖xd2 loses) 18...♗d6, and the c4 square becomes very weak.

17...♗a7 18.♖ac1 ♕b6

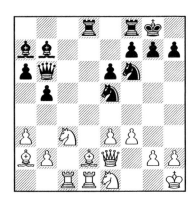

At first glance, white has literally no useful moves – total zugzwang! What can he do? He can't even create a luft – this will weaken the king. The spectators were sure that black would soon win. But after a long think, Reshevsky played

19.♘b1!

Amazing! The second knight is also evacuated from the front lines! White's plan is rather concrete: he intends to play 20.♗b4 and 21.♘c2, defusing the tension along the d-file. The trick 19...♘h5 20.♗b4 ♘f4 gives nothing due to 21.♕f1! Petrovs decided to prevent the immediate ♗b4.

19...♘d5?!

An inaccuracy: this move doesn't stop white from completing his regrouping, and there are no additional pieces to create pressure on e3. Actually, white had only one real weakness – the c4 square. Of course, it's a pity to trade the "good" b7 bishop for the "poor" a2 one, but after 19...♗d5! 20.♗xd5 ♘xd5 21.♘c2 ♘c4 the black cavalry seizes the coveted square. I don't doubt that Reshevsky would have entombed his own poor bishop on a2 with 20.b3! There's nothing forced here for black, but he would probably have a long-term initiative.

20.♘c2 ♘g6 21.♘c3

It's simply fantastic! One concession by the opponent, and white already achieves equality. It was extremely hard to defeat

Reshevsky in his best years: the American seemed to have nine lives!

21...♗b8   22.♘xd5   ♗xd5 23.♗xd5   ♖xd5   24.♗e1!   ♖xd1 25.♖xd1   ♖d8   26.♖xd8+   ♕xd8 27.♕d2 ♕xd2 28.♗xd2

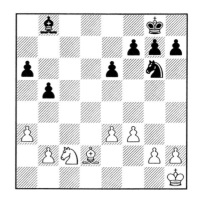

White offered a draw here. But Petrovs refused: the flag on Reshevsky's clock was already starting to rise, and the b2 and a3 pawns were on the squares of the same color as his bishop!

28...♗e5?!

A time-trouble trap that only serves to cede the last crumbs of advantage that black had. If he really wanted to play for a win, he needed to play 28...♘e5 29.♔g1 ♘c4 30.♗c3 ♗d6 — there is still some trouble ahead for white, even though Reshevsky would most probably have reached time control by getting his king to the queenside, and, considering his tenacity, the game would have probably ended in a draw.

29.b3 ♗b2 30.a4 ♘e5 31.♔g1!

Petrovs wanted to catch his opponent after 31.♘b4? a5 32.♘c2 b4, and the black knight is heading for the b3 pawn! However, this was too simple for such a master of time-trouble blitz as Reshevsky.

31...♔f8 32.♔f1 ♔e8 33.♔e2

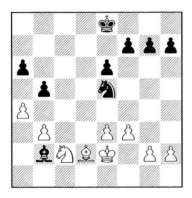

33...♔d7?

White had literally seconds on his clock, and the Latvian grandmaster lost his sense of danger. There was a simple draw after 33...♘c6, but black thought that white couldn't put his knight on b4.

34.♘b4!

The mirage has evaporated! 34...a5 is met with the brutal 35.♘d3!, and black is forced to go for a difficult bishop endgame: 35...♘xd3 36.♔xd3 b4 37.♔c4 ♔c6. Perhaps he should have played that anyway – it's not that simple for white to create a second weakness. However, Petrovs, like in his game against the world champion, gave up a pawn, hoping that his active pieces would give him a chance.

34...bxa4 35.bxa4 a5 36.♘d3 ♘c4 37.♗xa5 ♗f6 38.♗b4 ♔c6 39.e4! ♘b6 40.e5 ♗d8 41.♘b2, and when the game was resumed after adjournment, Reshevsky showed excellent technique and converted his advantage into a full point.

A heavy blow at the start! In addition to the loss, Vladimirs Petrovs caught a cold – it was chilly in Semmering, and the distraught grandmaster decided to take a walk without a coat. His body, weakened by long illness, reacted immediately, and his temperature rose to 38⁰C. In round 2, Petrovs played poorly in the opening against Capablanca and got a dangerous position, but it seemed that the great Cuban's goal was to make a quiet draw with black, and he achieved that goal without much effort.

And so, the leader of Latvian chess went to his game against Flohr with high hopes. Petrovs elegantly parried the Czech grandmaster's efforts to play for a win, a threefold repetition seemed inevitable, but the Riga player suddenly thought that he had some winning chances, pushed too hard and lost.

The second blow didn't knock him out either. Vladimirs Petrovs staggered, but continued to fight.

Game 20
V. Petrovs – P. Keres
Semmering-Baden 1937, round 4

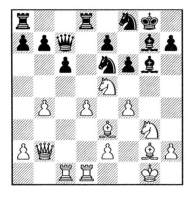

Black has been completely outplayed; Petrovs played positions with the king's bishop fianchetto brilliantly. The easiest way to win was a simple blow 22.♘xc6! bxc6 23.♖xc6 ♕d7 24.f5, and Keres could just resign. However, Vladimirs missed this tactical opportunity.

22.♘xg6 hxg6 23.f5 ♘f4

White's advantage was so overwhelming that even now his position is still close to won – the only thing he needed to do was to prevent the knight from reaching the blockading d5 square. After 24.♕b3+ ♔h8 25.d5! ♘xg2 26.♔xg2, the evaluation was defined by the horrible position of the f8 knight and g7 bishop. However, after **24.♗f3 ♘d5 25.♕b3 e6!**, black managed to stabilize the situation. Petrovs, frustrated by this turn of events, completely lost control over his position in time trouble, and white soon lost.

The grandmaster was in a state of shock. He wrote a letter to his wife, begging her to come as soon as possible (excerpts are provided in Part II of this book).

Alas, he couldn't "make a quiet draw" against Fine the next day that he promised his wife in his letter: there now followed Petrovs' worst game in his entire career.

Game 21
R. Fine – V. Petrovs
Semmering-Baden 1937, round 5
Queen's Pawn Game

1.d4 ♘f6 2.c4 b6?! 3.f3 ♗b7 4.e4 e5? 5.dxe5 ♘xe4 6.fxe4 ♕h4+ 7.♔d2 ♕f4+ 8.♔c2 ♗xe4+ 9.♗d3, and it's time for black to resign...

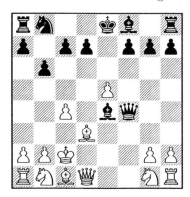

In round 6, the Latvian slowly outplayed Ragozin with black in the English opening, but again made some mistakes in time trouble and couldn't save the game after the adjournment. His score was 0.5/6! Petrovs lagged way behind all the other players and was incredibly anxious, fearing that nobody would ever invite him to a strong tournament again after such a performance. Thankfully, his wife went to Baden immediately after receiving his letter. And her arrival gave the suffering soul of the grandmaster some much needed peace.

Game 22
V. Petrovs – E. Eliskases
Semmering-Baden 1937, round 7

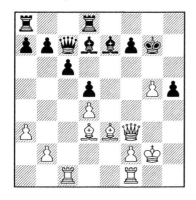

The Austrian player had 1.5/6, just a point ahead of Petrovs. Vladimirs wanted to climb out of clear last place and did everything he could to achieve that goal. White's kingside attack is in full swing, but how should he continue? Neither 23.♕xh5? ♖h8 nor 23.♖h1 ♗g4 is satisfactory. There's only one line that leads to success, and white had to anticipate a quiet move there.

23.♗f4 ♗d6

Eliskases had counted on 24.♗xd6 ♕xd6, and black is better, but that was just a dream.

24.♗g3! ♗g4

Black's position is already bad. 24...♗e6 didn't help either: 25.♕f6+ ♔g8 26.♕h6, and black is doomed.

25.♕f6+ ♔g8 26.♕h6 f5 27.gxf6 ♕f7 28.♗e5 ♗xe5 29.dxe5 ♖d7 30.f3 ♕e6 31.♕g5+. Black resigned.

After the first leg, the standings were as follows: 1. Keres – 5/7 points, 2. Fine – 4.5, 3–5. Capablanca, Flohr, Reshevsky – 4, 6. Ragozin – 3.5, 7–8. Petrovs, Eliskases – 1.5.

Game 23
V. Petrovs – S. Reshevsky
Semmering-Baden 1937, round 8

At the start of the second leg, Petrovs again faced Reshevsky. The American had already defeated Vladimirs twice despite having very difficult positions, and the Riga player wanted to finally take his revenge. He again got a huge advantage, but Reshevsky defended with only moves, creating a fortress-like structure. Petrovs found more and more resources, the game was adjourned twice, and black finally slipped up on move 75!

White's position also has some weaknesses – he has to watch the a4 and e4 pawns closely, and had Reshevsky now played 75...♕f7, the walls of his "citadel" would have remained solid and impregnable. But black had long planned to transfer his knight to d6, and he finally decided that the time had come.

75...♘e8?

This allows for some spectacular geometry. How can white win? Petrovs solves this puzzle in a brilliant way.

76.♕h2!

The e5 pawn is attacked, and if black defends it with his king, 76...♔d6, the incredible 77.♔e3! follows, threatening ♕b2, and 77...♘f6 is met with 78.♕xe5+!!, when the queen cannot be captured because of mate in one. Reshevsky finds the most tenacious reply, but even that can't save him.

76...♕f7

76...♘d6   77.♕xe5   ♘xc4 78.♕e7+ ♔c8 79.♗f4 loses, but now the queen is ready to jump to h5 from f7, and so white has to make a prophylactic king move.

77.♔d3 ♔d6 78.♕b2! ♕b7

79.♗d2?!

A small inaccuracy. Petrovs saw that he could win a pawn and lost an opportunity to create a masterpiece. After the elegant 79.♗h4, white could still sacrifice his queen. Black cannot allow 80.♗g3, and 79...♘f6 is met with the familiar 80.♕xe5+!!

79...♘f6

Black cannot retreat with his queen due to 80.♗c3, and after losing the a5 pawn, it's just hopeless.

80.♗xa5 ♘d7 81.♕b5 ♕c7 82.♗d2 ♕c8 83.♗g5 ♕a8 84.♔c2 ♕c8 85.a5 bxa5 86.♕xa5 ♕b8 87.♕d8 ♕xd8 88.♗xd8, and white easily won after 102 moves by going for the g7 pawn with his king. An emphatic victory!

Eliskases also won (against Ragozin), and so the stragglers were catching up: 1. Keres – 6, 2. Fine – 5, 3. Capablanca – 4.5, 4–5. Flohr, Reshevsky – 4, 6. Ragozin – 3.5, 7–8. Petrovs, Eliskases – 2.5. In round 9, Petrovs easily drew with Capablanca with black and escaped last place – Eliskases lost to Reshevsky. Moreover, Ragozin lost to Keres, and Vladimirs could even harbor some hopes for sixth place – he was just half a point behind the Soviet player. However, the Austrian grandmaster then caught a wave of luck: he defeated Keres from a poor position, then ground down Capablanca in a long endgame, while Petrovs blundered a central pawn to the Estonian... Before the last round,

Ragozin and Eliskases were a whole point ahead, and he couldn't catch up: the Soviet grandmaster saved the game against Flohr, and the head-to-head encounter with Eliskases was drawn. As a result, Petrovs finished last – for the only time in his career: 1. Keres – 9, 2. Fine – 8, 3–4. Reshevsky, Capablanca – 7.5, 5. Flohr – 7, 6–7. Ragozin, Eliskases – 6, 8. Petrovs – 5.

The Latvian grandmaster immediately rushed into battle again, trying to prove that his setback in Baden was just an accident. In early 1938, Austria was annexed by Germany (the Anschluss), and a tournament with the strongest German and Austrian players was organized in the German resort town of Bad Harzburg, with two foreign luminaries invited – Vladimirs Petrovs and Vasja Pirc of Yugoslavia. Petrovs started with draws against Grandmaster Friedrich Samisch, the inventor of various systems with f2-f3, and Master Josef Lokvenc, and then defeated August Preusse.

Game 24
V. Petrovs – A. Preusse
Bad Harzburg 1938, round 3
Slav Defense

1.♘f3 d5 2.c4 c6 3.b3 ♘f6 4.♗b2 ♗f5 5.g3 e6 6.♗g2 ♗d6 7.0-0 h6 8.d4 ♘bd7 9.♘bd2 0-0 10.♘e5 ♗xe5 11.dxe5 ♘g4 12.♘f3 ♗e4 13.♕d4 c5 14.♕d2 d4 15.♖fd1

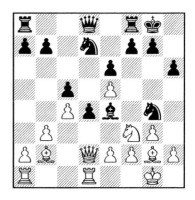

At first glance, black's position looks very good: the b2 bishop is out of play, and he will soon grab the lonely e5 pawn. The German player thought that as well, but it turned out that white is actually threatening to take on d4 – with both bishop and knight!

For instance, after 15...♕b8, white obtains an advantage with 16.♗xd4 cxd4 17.♕xd4 ♗xf3 18.exf3 ♘xf2 (18...♘gxe5 19.f4 loses a pawn) 19.♕xf2 ♕xe5 20.f4. 15...♗xf3!? 16.♗xf3 ♘dxe5 17.♗xb7 ♖b8 18.♗g2 would have been a good alternative: black is slightly worse, but his opponent will have a hard time getting his b2 bishop into play. Preusse, however, missed white's cunning plan and put his queen on c7.

15...♕c7?

Counting on 16.♗xd4 cxd4 17.♕xd4 ♘c5 18.b4 ♖ac8 19.bxc5 ♕xc5 20.♕xe4 ♘xf2 21.♕d4 ♘xd1 22.♕xc5 ♖xc5 23.♖xd1 ♖xc4 with a complicated endgame. However, trouble came from another side.

16.♘xd4! ♗xg2 17.♘b5 ♕c6 18.♕xd7 ♕xd7 19.♖xd7 ♗c6

20.♖c7, and Petrovs easily converted his extra pawn.

In round 4, the Latvian grandmaster had a dramatic duel with his old acquaintance Kurt Richter – he got a difficult endgame with two pawns for the exchange but a poor pawn structure, then he managed to outplay his opponent but missed the win in a rook endgame. The next game was also drawn – Petrovs defended a worse position against Eliskases. After five rounds, Pirc was in the lead with 4 points, trailed by Georg Kieninger (3.5), and third place was shared by Petrovs, Eliskases and Bogoljubov. The time had come for Petrovs to face the former world championship challenger.

Game 25
E. Bogoljubov – V. Petrovs
Bad Harzburg 1938, round 6
Slav Defense

In the 1920s and early 1930s, Efim Dmitrievich Bogoljubov was one of the strongest players in the world: he won two Soviet Championships and later, settling in Germany for good, played two world championship matches against Alekhine, where he fared poorly. In 1938, however, Bogoljubov was already declining. His age (49) started to show, and in the eyes of the Nazis, the former candidate had an unavoidable flaw: he wasn't "Aryan". Because of that, he often had to miss large tournaments in Germany, and never represented his team at the Olympiad during the Nazi era. According to Fyodor Bogatyrchuk, Bogoljubov even joined the Nazi Party during the war in an effort to ease his situation somewhat.

Still, Bogoljubov commanded huge authority in the chess world; shortly after this tournament, he played a match against Eliskases for the title of the absolute champion of unified Germany (Erich Eliskases won it rather confidently, 11.5–8.5).

Efim Dmitrievich was considered a very dangerous player with white – even in his matches against Alekhine, where he was crushed with black, he still managed to regularly pose problems for the world champion with white. However, Petrovs stunned his opponent with a new idea and easily won the opening duel against the renowned opening expert and advocate of 1.d2-d4.

1.d4 d5 2.♘f3 ♘f6 3.c4 c6 4.♘c3 dxc4 5.a4 ♗f5 6.e3 e6 7.♗xc4 ♗b4 8.0–0 0–0 9.♘h4

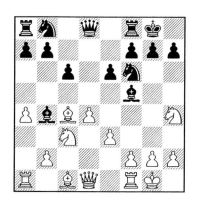

Back then, this was a new move in top-level chess; the main line was 9.♕e2, as Euwe played against Alekhine. The knight jump had though already been played by Asztalos against Tarrasch, and after 9...♗g6 10.♘xg6 hxg6 11.♕e2, the famous grandmaster and author of numerous aphorisms quickly got a poor position. But Petrovs' reply shocked Bogoljubov to the core: the Riga player didn't even bother to retreat!

9...♘bd7!

One of the first games that used this system of development (and the very first in this line). Black gives up his light-squared bishop, but he's counting on his pawn barricades to limit the activity of his opponent's minor pieces and on his knights easily seizing the d5 square.

10.♘xf5 exf5

Later, this line occurred in the game Botvinnik – Smyslov (World Championship 1954), and Mikhail Moiseevich, who knew the source game and played two closed training games against Kan in the variation, preferred 10.f3 ♗g6 11.e4 e5 12.♘xg6 hxg6 13.♗e3 ♕e7, winning in a sharp struggle, which almost rendered Petrovs' idea obsolete. Interestingly, one of the first players who showed that black's position still had its merits was Yuri Dokhoian in the 1980s! And a couple of years later, the whole chess elite started playing this line. However, in 1938, Bogoljubov just couldn't believe

his eyes: such positional audacity! And, with characteristic optimism, he started to "refute" his opponent's experiment.

11.♕f3?! g6 12.h3 h5 13.♕f4

The blow against the black pawn chain didn't connect, so Bogoljubov decides to get his queen to h6 and try to create a threat of capture on g6.

13...♘b6   14.♗b3   ♘bd5 15.♕h6?? ♖e8 16.f3 ♗f8?!

Here, black could immediately trap the stray queen: 16...♘g4! 17.fxg4 ♗f8, winning. Still, even after the game move, Bogoljubov's position falls apart at the seams.

17.♕g5   ♗g7   18.♗d2   ♕b6 19.♗c4?

19.♘xd5 ♘xd5 20.♗xd5 cxd5 doesn't look pretty either, but the trade on d5 at least prevented immediate material losses.

19...♘h7!

The e3 square falls, and white's position falls with it.

20.♕h4 ♘xe3 21.♗xe3 ♖xe3 22.♖ad1 ♕xb2 23.♘e4 ♕b4 24.♕f4 ♕xc4 25.♕xe3 fxe4 26.fxe4 ♖e8

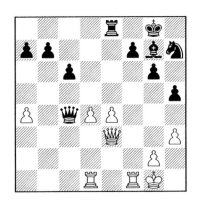

Before tournaments, Volodya suffered from a lack of sleep. If he lost a game, he wouldn't close his eyes all night and would smoke abundantly, suffering greatly. I had to calm and comfort him like a child. Sometimes I really had enough of it. And then I would implore him to abandon this "nasty chess" that did nothing but ruin his life. "Look, you're a trained lawyer, try to become a good barrister"

I would have liked so much to write "etc." here: black has two pieces and a pawn for a rook, and the rest is technical, but Petrovs later played imprecisely and missed the win... Alas, Vladimirs Petrovs' form was still far from perfect.

The grandmaster played irresolutely against Pirc and lost a pawn in the opening, but a draw was enough for the Yugoslavian player to keep his lead, and so he agreed to a three-fold repetition. In the penultimate round, Petrovs got a better endgame against Kieninger, but played inaccurately and missed the transition to a drawn rook endgame. Before the last round, Pirc led with 6/8, trailed by Bogoljubov and Kieninger (5/8), Petrovs (4.5/8), and Eliskases, Lokvenc and Heinicke (4/8 each). Pirc made a short draw with Lokvenc, Kieninger barely managed to survive against Samisch, Bogoljubov defeated Preusse, Eliskases brought down Ritter, and Petrovs suffered a true tragedy.

Game 26
V. Petrovs – H. Heinicke
Bad Harzburg 1938, round 9

Game 27
G. Stahlberg – V. Petrovs
Lodz 1938

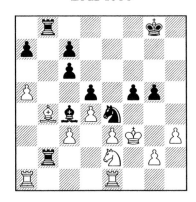

Petrovs has mounted a beautiful attack with sacrifices, and after the simple 36.♕c2 (or 36.♕e2) 36...♖xd4 37.♕xa2+ e6 38.♖xe6, Herbert Heinicke's position would have fallen apart. However, the grandmaster thought that **36.♘f3??** created an unstoppable threat ♗h3, overlooking the reply **36...e5!**

After **37.♗h3 ♕c6 38.♕e3 ♖gd8** white lost a lot of material, and Vladimirs only finished on a 50% score.

In the next tournament, the Riga player was more successful. At the Lodz event, Petrovs faced Pirc, Tartakower, Stahlberg, Najdorf and Eliskases. Pirc continued his winning streak with 11.5/15, Tartakower took second place with 10/15, and third place was shared by Eliskases, Petrovs and Stahlberg; the Swedish grandmaster, who had just drawn a match with Paul Keres (4–4), lost to Petrovs with white in just 27 moves.

White is completely paralyzed, and the threat 27...♗xe2+ and 28... g4+ is unstoppable. Stahlberg played **27.h4** and stopped the clock as soon as Petrovs removed the white knight from the board.

Meanwhile, Alexander Alekhine brilliantly defeated Max Euwe in the return match, and, after some rest, decided to take part in the Margate tournament that also included Golombek, Menchik, Alexander, Sergeant, Petrovs, Milner-Barry, Book, Thomas and Spielmann. The champion quickly got down to business, winning four games in a row. However, the streak was broken in round 5.

Petrovs enjoyed a good start with 2.5/3, defeating Sergeant and Golombek, but his experiment in round 4 failed: he played the Scheveningen system against Alexander and lost. Therefore, he played a very solid Catalan against the world champion.

Game 28
V. Petrovs – A. Alekhine
Margate 1938, round 5
Catalan Opening

1.d4 ♘f6 2.c4 e6 3.g3 d5 4.♗g2 dxc4 5.♕a4+ ♘bd7 6.♘f3 a6 7.♘c3 ♖b8 8.♕xc4 b5 9.♕d3 ♗b7 10.0-0 c5 11.dxc5 ♘xc5 12.♕xd8+ ♖xd8 13.♗f4 b4 14.♘d1 ♘d5 15.♖c1 ♘xf4 16.gxf4 ♗d6 17.♘e5 ♗xg2 18.♔xg2

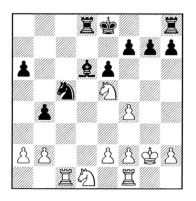

In this position, the d1 knight is out of play, but black needs to counter the threat ♘e5-c6. Alekhine solves the threat in the most radical way.

18...b3! 19.axb3 f6?!

But this is imprecise. Alexander Alekhine thinks that the white pawns aren't going anywhere and chases the white knight, but 19...♘xb3! 20.♖c6 g5 or 20...♘d4 was stronger – black has some micro-plus, but there's too little material left on the board, and white has good drawing chances.

20.♘c6 ♖c8

Funnily enough, some sources suggested that black could get an advantage with 20...♘xb3 21.♘xd8 ♘xc1 22.♘xe6 ♔f7 23.♘d4? ♗xf4. White's dynamics are so well-hidden that his position got underestimated by both Alekhine and the commentators. After the strongest 23.f5! ♘xe2 24.♔f3! ♘c1 25.♘e3 ♘b3 (25...♘d3 26.♖d1 ♘e5+ 27.♔e4 is no better) 26.♖d1 ♗e7 27.♖d7, white is close to winning, so black's move was correct.

21.♘d4 ♔d7?! Another step towards the abyss. As in a later game against Fine at the AVRO tournament, Alekhine relies upon the weakness of his opponent's pawns and sends his king towards the center, getting under fire from the numerous enemy pieces. After the modest 21...♔f7 22.e3 ♖b8 23.♘c3 ♘xb3 24.♘xb3 ♖xb3 25.♘e4, the game was most likely drawn. Black probably wanted to get his king closer to the important events after 22.e3, but he was up for a big surprise!

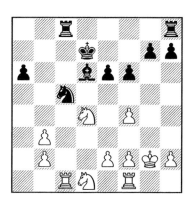

22.♘e3! ♗xf4 23.♖fd1

Black can create two pairs of doubled pawns in white's position, but how to defend against tactical threats?

23...♔e7?

And this is a mistake! The discovered check is not dangerous, and after the cold-blooded 23... ♘e4! 24.♖a1 ♗xe3 25.fxe3 ♖a8 26.♘f5+ ♔e8 27.♘xg7+ ♔e7, white's shattered pawns give him no winning chances. But why is the king move so bad?

24.b4! ♗xe3?

Alekhine could still have saved the game with the tactical trick 24... ♘a4 25.♖xc8 ♖xc8 26.♖a1 ♗e5!, but he hoped to win.

25.fxe3 ♘d7 26.♖a1!

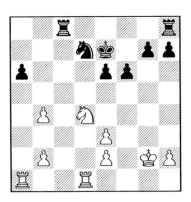

An incredible position! White's pawn structure is completely broken, and black's one is ideal, but Alekhine can't save the game because his pieces cannot regroup in time, and the a6 pawn is doomed!

26...♘b8 27.b5 axb5 28.♖a7+ ♔d6 29.♘xb5+ ♔c5 30.♘d6 ♖c6 31.b4+!

31.♘e4+ ♔b6 32.♖xg7 also won, but Petrovs chose a beautiful and technical line.

31...♔xb4   32.♖b7+   ♔c3 33.♘c4+ ♔c2 34.♖bb1

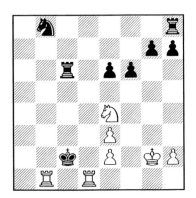

Checkmate is inevitable, and Alekhine resigned. It's hard to remember another game where the fourth world champion was destroyed so comprehensively.

Before the last round, only the Latvian grandmaster could still challenge the world champion: 1. Alekhine – 6.5/8, 2. Petrovs – 5.5, 3–4. Spielmann, Book – 5. Alas, Vladimirs blundered against Spielmann in their head-to-head game and only took third place.

Back then, the Estonian team played regular matches against their neighbors – Lithuania, Latvia and Finland. In 1937, Estonia defeated Lithuania in a tense battle – 8.5–7.5, then, in 1938, they defeated Finland 9.6–6.5, and finally, they invited their strongest rival in the Baltic region, Latvia. This time, the Estonians couldn't win: the guests won by a three-point margin, with Petrovs bringing down Keres, 1.5–0.5!

Game 29
V. Petrovs – P. Keres
Tallinn 1938, round 2
(Latvia – Estonia)

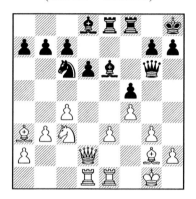

Keres risked the Dutch Defense, but got under pressure. It's now time to convert the advantages, so Petrovs chose the energetic **21.c5! dxc5 22.♗xc5 ♗e7 23.♗xe7 ♖xe7 24.♗xc6! bxc6 25.♕d4**. White's advantage was huge. "Paul Petrovich" put up tough resistance, but the Latvian leader ground down his opponent in a long rook ending.

The result of the match as a whole and on first board specifically was a big blow for the Estonians. Does

that mean that Vladimirs Petrovs was the strongest player of the entire Baltic region? Well, the teams met again the following year, and Estonia exacted revenge – 10–6. Paul Keres also managed to even the score.

Game 30
P. Keres – V. Petrovs
Riga 1939, round 1
(Estonia – Latvia)

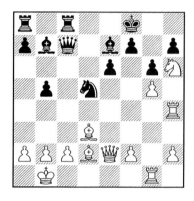

Black's play in the French Defense had been quite poor, and he got quickly punished for that: **23.♘xf7!**, after which Keres destroyed his opponent's kingside. In the second game, Petrovs decided to play for a draw, but his play was hesitant, he missed a break in the center and lost again. The leader of Estonian chess thus had his personal revenge.

The Last Olympiad

Petrovs' woes continued into 1939. After losing badly to Keres, he played poorly in Kemeri as well. It was disappointing to take such a low place at the same venue where he had scored his most impressive victory, even though the line-up was more modest this time... Vladimirs lost five games, four of them to the top four – Flohr, Mikenas, Stahlberg and Szabo. A perfect score against the tail-enders (6/6) was poor consolation for the results against grandmasters; Petrovs took 8th place with a +1 score.

But there was no time for sadness: the Latvian team was heading for the Olympiad in Argentina.

The Tournament of Nations was held outside Europe for the first time in its history, a lot of teams were expected to participate, and so the round-robin format was scrapped in favor of four groups, with the top 4 teams from each group progressing to the main final. The first board "mini-tournament" line-up was quite impressive: Alekhine, Capablanca, Keres, Petrovs, Eliskases, Stahlberg, Mikenas, and Tartakower. Only Flohr (the leading Czech grandmaster had emigrated to the USSR after Czechoslovakia was occupied by Germany) and Reshevsky were missing – the American team didn't go to Argentina. Consequently,

the Olympiad main prize, the Hamilton-Russell Cup, remained in the Marshall Club in New York. When the organizers demanded the return of the valuable trophy, the winners of the Stockholm edition refused, saying that as three-time Olympiad winners, they had the right to keep it forever. A conflict on the level of embassies ensued, and the Cup was ultimately delivered to the Olympiad.

But this conflict was far from the only one at the tournament. Before the group stage, the German captain (or, more precisely, the captain of the "Third Reich team") demanded that Czechoslovakia change its flag to that of "Protectorate of Bohemia and Moravia". The Czechs vehemently refused, and other teams supported their decision. The Czech tricolor hung on the stage until the end of the tournament. The semi-finals started, and all the strongest teams indeed progressed to the final: Poland, Czechoslovakia, England and Brazil from Group 1, Argentina, Lithuania, Netherlands and Denmark from Group 3, Sweden, Estonia, Palestine and Cuba from Group 4. The Latvian team played in Group 2 and confidently took first place! Petrovs' team featured all its strongest players this time, and, to the surprise of many chess fans, ended ahead of Germany, Chile and France in that group.

Vladimirs Petrovs' play at the qualifying stage was restrained: he intentionally drew against Alekhine and Eliskases, defeated the players from Bolivia and Chile, and drew against Uruguay and Bulgaria. All this didn't matter anyway: the qualifying stage performance had no bearing on the results of the final stage, either individual or team.

The first round of the final started on 1st September 1939 in Buenos Aires. In the middle of the games, someone brought horrible news: Germany had invaded Poland. Britain declared war on Germany two days later and the English team left the tournament and went home – only 15 teams remained at the final stage. That same evening, Alexander Alekhine made a speech on the radio and spoke to national Argentinian newspapers, demanding a boycott of the German team. The Olympiad was in jeopardy – most team captains supported Alekhine's ultimatum at the general assembly. The organizers made an effort to persuade the others not to kick Germany out, but France and Poland adamantly refused to play against Eliskases' team. Those matches were declared drawn 2–2. Germany, in turn, coerced Czechoslovakia to withdraw from the France and Poland matches as well – these were also declared drawn 2–2.

After long deliberations, the final tournament continued, but then another conflict arose: Palestine also refused to play against Germany. The German team demanded that the match be declared 4–0 in their favor, insisting that drawing a weak team was not in their plans. No progress had been made until Argentina, who started with three wins and had great prospects, made a sacrifice – they offered Germany to agree to a 2–2 draw with Palestine on condition that Argentina agreed to a draw with Palestine, too. A compromise was found: Eliskases' team was still in hot pursuit of the hosts, and so the compromise suited them. The organizers managed to save the Olympiad in a tense situation.

The Latvian team started the finals with a draw against the Netherlands; Petrovs drew with Van Scheltinga (Max Euwe didn't travel to Buenos Aires). In round 2, Latvia won a match against Estonia, 2.5–1.5 (this time, the encounter Keres – Petrovs quickly reached the endgame, and the Latvian leader easily drew), and in round 3, they defeated Lithuania 3–1, with Petrovs winning against Mikenas. Two victories in the Baltic derbies boosted the team's morale, but then a cold shower ensued – Latvia lost three matches in a row: to Czechoslovakia (0.5–3.5), Germany (1–3) and Argentina (1.5–2.5). Something had to be done, and Petrovs took the lead.

Game 31
V. Petrovs – O. Trompowsky
Buenos Aires 1939, round 7
(Latvia – Brazil)

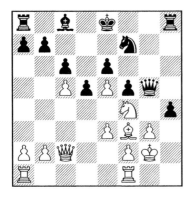

Brazilian chess player Octavio Trompowsky was a creative and original player; for instance, he developed the famous 1.d4 ♘f6 2.♗g5 opening. The position on the board is difficult and complicated. Black hasn't developed the c8 bishop or a8 rook, preferring to immediately mount a kingside attack. Petrovs decides to fight fire with fire, logically surmising that white's development advantage should play a role.

22.♖h1! hxg3?

The point of white's plan is that black cannot capture the e5 pawn: 22...♘xe5 23.♕c3 ♘f7 24.♗h5! ♖xh5 25.♘xh5 ♕xh5 26.♖xh4 ♕g6 27.♖h8+ ♔e7 (27...♘xh8 28.♕xh8+ ♔e7 29.♖h1 leads to a quick rout) 28.♖ah1, and the second rook goes to h7. Here, black needed to remember his queenside – 22...♗d7!; for instance, after 23.♗h5 ♖xh5 24.♘xh5 ♕xh5 25.♖xh4 ♕g6, all three results are

still possible. However, Trompowsky committed positional suicide by opening the h-file too early.

23.♖xh8+ ♘xh8 24.♖h1 ♘f7

24...gxf2+ 25.♔xf2 ♘f7 26.♗h5 doesn't help.

25.♗h5!

And here's the punishment: the black bishop and rook will never enter play. The end.

25...♕g7 26.♗g6 ♗d7 27.♖h7 ♕xe5 28.♗xf7+ ♔d8 29.♕c3

Black resigned, and Latvia won 2.5–1.5 against Brazil.

In round 8, the Baltic team faced France, and Petrovs was supposed to have white against Alekhine, but Vladimirs didn't get to face the world champion again. The reason was as follows: Alekhine's main rival, Capablanca, had recorded a flying start in the first rounds of the finals (in the semi-finals, the great Cuban only defeated a Guatemalan player, drawing all other games), crushed Czerniak and Van Scheltinga and destroyed Mikenas in 26 moves. The world champion seriously feared that Capablanca would win gold for first board and then assert his moral right to a return match once again. Alexander Alexandrovich knew all too well that he would most likely draw with Petrovs, which would deprive him of any chance to catch Capablanca. In the first rounds, the champion faced strong opponents: Stahlberg, Keres, Mikenas; he hadn't won a single game yet, and he was way behind Capa. And so, Alekhine offered the following to the Latvian team: Petrovs doesn't play, but France's second-board player doesn't play either. This arrangement satisfied the Latvians: their lower boards were manned by masters or first-category players with rich tournament experience, whereas the majority of the French team comprised amateurs. Apsenieks played first board, and he traded on d5 on the third move of the French Defense. The world champion flashed his eyes in anger; he did eventually win after a long endgame, but Latvia won the match – 2.5–1.5.

After a rest day, Petrovs continued to score points: he precisely converted his advantage against Enevoldsen, calmly defended against Capablanca and defeated Tartakower.

Game 32
V. Petrovs – S. Tartakower
Buenos Aires 1939, round 12
(Latvia – Poland)

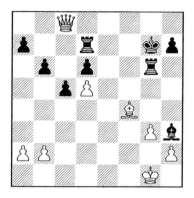

Black has two rooks for the queen, and his bishop on h3 is waiting to

Buenos Aries Chess Olympiad, September 1939

weave a mating net for the white king. But it's Petrovs' turn, and white has enough time to target the opposing monarch first.

35.♗d2!

Now 35...♗g4 loses after 36.♕e8!, but Tartakower's move was no better.

35...♖f6?

Black's only chance was 35... h6! 36.♗c3+ (there was a beautiful trap: 36.♕e8 ♖f7 37.♗c3+ ♖gf6, threatening mate on f1) 36...♔f7 37.♕h8 ♗f5, but after 38.♔f2 ♖e7 39.h4! white kept the initiative.

36.♗c3 ♔f7 37.♗xf6 ♔xf6 38.♕h8+

Alas, black has no hope of creating a fortress: passive defense allows the white king to reach f4, and the attempt to capture the d5 pawn leads to the bishop's loss.

38...♔f5 39.♔f2 ♔e4 40.♕e8+ ♔xd5 41.♕h5+ ♔c6 42.♕xh3, and white won, saving the match which ended 2–2.

In round 12, another incident happened that poured even more gasoline onto the fire at the tournament. Capablanca easily reached a +4 score and then decided to avoid any risks – first of all, he skipped a game against Keres with black. After a white game against Petrovs, the Cuban had to face another ordeal: a black game against his historical rival. Alekhine won another game in the meantime, and if he defeated Capa as well, he could catch up with the leader. However,

when the line-ups were announced, it turned out that Alberto Lopez, Cuba's reserve player, had taken first board. The world champion was infuriated and won in 25 moves, and then said many unflattering things about his predecessor on the throne...

Other competitors also caught up, and the situation before the last round was incredibly tense: Eliskases had scored 6/8 (75%), Capablanca 7.5/10 (75%), Petrovs 9/12 (75%), Stahlberg 8/11 (73%), Alekhine 6.5/9 (72%), and Keres 9/13 (69%). The chess world hadn't seen such a battle for first board gold in the entire history of the Olympiads! The situation in the team tournament was very sharp as well: 1. Germany – 34 points, 2–3. Poland, Estonia – 32, 4. Sweden – 31.5, 5–6. Argentina, Czechoslovakia – 30, 7. Latvia 29, 8. Netherlands 28.5. The last round pairings were as follows: Germany – Netherlands, Poland – Denmark (who were last in the table), Estonia – Argentina, Sweden – Latvia and Czechoslovakia – Lithuania; the first board standings were to be decided in the games Van Scheltinga – Eliskases, Stahlberg – Petrovs, Capablanca – Trompowsky, Czerniak – Alekhine and Keres – Piazzini.

The Politeama Theater was packed to the brim before the decisive battles. Some spectators arrived early in the morning – everyone wanted to see which famous grandmaster would prevail. More than three thousand tickets were sold. The South Americans met the chess gladiators on stage with loud ovations, and the fight started! Keres, Capablanca and Alekhine quickly dispatched their opponents, while Eliskases failed to defeat the Dutch master and lost his chance to finish in the top three. And now, everything depended on the duel between Stahlberg and Petrovs – this was the last important game in the Buenos Aires Olympiad! After some middlegame complications, the opponents went for a complex endgame. Other games had finished, but Gideon and Vladimirs continued their battle. The Swedish grandmaster desperately needed to win: it would allow his team to catch up with Estonia, who had stumbled against Argentina, and Stahlberg himself would thus take the individual silver, ahead of Alekhine. For Petrovs, it was simple: a draw guaranteed an individual bronze.

Game 33
G. Stahlberg – V. Petrovs
Buenos Aires 1939, round 15
(Sweden – Latvia)

The last game in Buenos Aries, 1939. In his career, Petrovs played Alekhine five times, with an overall score of 2.5-2.5

The position was drawish, and after 56.♔f4 ♞h3+, they could have repeated. Stahlberg made one last desperate attempt to win, but it turned out to be too risky.

56.♔h4? ♞f3+ 57.♔h5

It's hard to judge what white was counting on – maybe 57...♞d2 58.♖e6? Even after 57...♜xe3 58.♞xe3 ♔f6, the position is still drawn. However, the white king's position on the edge of the board gave Petrovs a hidden chance.

57...♞d4?

Black could have punished his opponent for his recklessness with 57...♞e5! 58.♞xe5+ dxe5 59.♖xe5: after the Zwischenzug 59...♔f6!, white loses due to the mate threat 60.♖e1 (both 60.♖e8 ♔xf5 61.♔h6 ♖xa3 62.♖b8 ♖a1 63.♖xb6 a3 and 60.♖e6+ ♔xf5 lead to disaster) 60...♔xf5 61.♖f1+ ♔e4 62.♖a1 ♔d4, and all Stahlberg's pawns fall. Now, however, a draw is inevitable.

58.♔g5 ♖xe3 59.♞xe3 b5 60.cxb5 ♞xb5 61.♞c4 ♔g7 62.f6+

♔f7, and, in view of 63.♔f5 ♞d4+ 64.♔g5 ♞b5, the opponents agreed to a draw.

Ultimately, the first-board gold was won by Capablanca. Alekhine came second, and Petrovs third, which was quite an achievement – unlike the world champions, Vladimirs Mikhailovich couldn't pick his opponents, "I'll play white with this guy, but I won't play black with that guy!" The Third Reich team won the Olympiad... and all of its members decided to remain in Argentina. Poland came second, Estonia kept their third place, and Petrovs' team finished seventh – of course, largely thanks to their leader! Vladimirs Petrovs again proved that he was one of the strongest players in the world, having played a brilliant tournament almost without dubious positions. Alas, his performance went largely unnoticed – Europe was burning, and nobody paid much attention to chess...

A Victim of Circumstances

The Buenos Aires Olympiad was now over, and the European participants faced a new challenge – how to get home? The Atlantic was becoming a battlefield between allied squadrons and the Nazi German fleet, and Karl Doenitz's Kriegsmarine was mercilessly sinking trading convoys, so passenger ships between South America and Europe became a rarity. A number of famous players (Keres, Stahlberg and Najdorf, who decided to stay in Argentina permanently) accepted the Argentinian organizers' proposal to play a 12-player exhibition tournament (1–2. Keres, Najdorf – 8.5/11, 3–4. Stahlberg, Czerniak – 7). Petrovs declined to take part and decided to go back to Latvia on the next steamship, *Copacabana*, which was due in a week. As he waited for the departure, the hero of the Olympiad moved to Rosario, where he played a small round-robin tournament together with Mikenas, Eliskases and five local players.

V. Petrovs – V. Mikenas
Rosario 1939

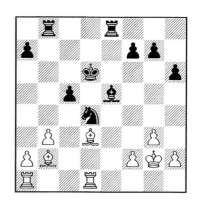

Vladas Mikenas had carelessly parted with his light-squared bishop in the Catalan and was now under strong pressure. After **27.♖ac1**, neither 27...♔c6 28.♗a3 ♗d6 29.♗c4! f6 30.♖xd4! cxd4 31.♗e6+ ♔b6 32.♗xd6 nor 27...♖bc8 28.♗a6 ♖c7 29.b4 saves black, so Petrovs' Baltic neighbor made a blunder characteristic of poor positions.

27...♖e7? 28.♖xc5! ♔xc5 29.♗a3+ ♔b6

Or 29...♖b4 30.♖c1+.

30.♗xe7 ♘c6 31.♗a3 ♖d8 32.♗e2 ♖xd1 33.♗xd1, and white won easily.

The result of this game had an impact on the whole tournament: Eliskases drew with Mikenas and Petrovs, and then Vladimirs Mikhailovich destroyed all the

Argentinian players and took first place with an impressive 6.5/7 score. After that, a long road home awaited him...

Petrovs returned to Latvia, which soon got annexed by the Soviet Union, placing a 25,000-strong military contingent in the Baltic country. Lithuania and Estonia were absorbed into the USSR too, which posed an unexpected question for Soviet chess officials: it would be only logical if the three strongest Baltic players (Keres, Petrovs and Mikenas) took part in the 1940 Soviet Championship, but how to do that if the line-up was already full? The number of participants was quickly increased from 18 to 20, but still, there was an odd man out...

"It turns out that fate played a very cruel joke on master Leonid Shamaev. He took second place, and in April the *64* newspaper named him among the participants of the 12th Soviet Championship. Two months later, in the bulletin of the Kiev semi-final, he was drawn as one of the passengers of the symbolic tram #12. But in the summer, Latvia, Lithuania and Estonia became parts of the Soviet Union, and their champions were obliged to take part in the country's main tournament. Someone had to be sacrificed, and for some reason, Shamaev's name was struck out – instead of

Ragozin, who took a lower place in the Leningrad championship... Shamaev wouldn't get a second chance to take part in such a competition." (Sergey Voronkov in *Masterpieces and Dramas of the Soviet Championships: Volume II (1938-1947)*, English version: Elk and Ruby, 2021.)

What hopes did Petrovs harbor for the upcoming tournament? How good was his form? On the one hand, most Soviet masters were completely unknown in the West, but on the other hand Vladimirs Petrovs remembered Paul Keres' performance at the 1939 Leningrad/Moscow training tournament quite well: the victor of the AVRO tournament and winner of a match with Euwe scored just 8/17, losing to Makogonov, Ragozin, Konstantinopolsky and Alatortsev! Of course, the leader of Latvian chess knew quite well how strong his opposition would be, but the maestro couldn't prepare for the tournament as well as he would have liked. He had played his last tournament game in Argentina more than a year before the Soviet Championship, and the conditions in the country sandwiched between Stalin's and Hitler's spheres of interests were by definition not conducive for preparation.

Interestingly, the three Baltic players were awarded very different titles by the Soviet Qualification Committee. Keres received the grandmaster title, Petrovs became a master, but they only gave the master's title to Mikenas in 1942... Of course, such a demotion offended Vladimirs Mikhailovich; Petrovs was called a grandmaster by the chess press of the whole world and the world champions Alexander Alekhine and Jose Raul Capablanca, but the Latvian champion had no doubt that the committee's decision was just a sad mistake, and he would soon be able to prove that he was worthy of the USSR grandmaster's title. By the way, only four grandmasters took part in that historical tournament: Mikhail Botvinnik, Paul Keres, Grigory Levenfish and Alexander Kotov, who had performed brilliantly in the previous All-Union championship (only his loss to Botvinnik in the last round deprived Kotov of the golden medal, which was won by his opponent). The first USSR grandmaster title was awarded in 1929 to maestro Boris Verlinsky for winning the national championship; however, later it was abolished for four years, and there was no place left for Verlinsky in the new hierarchy of high titles.

And so, Petrovs drew number 7 at the drawing ceremony, and in the first round, he faced the revelation of the previous championship – Grandmaster Alexander Kotov.

Game 35
V. Petrovs – A. Kotov
Moscow 1940, 12th Soviet Championship, round 1

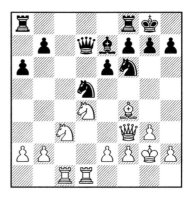

Another Catalan had given white a promising position, however, it's not quite clear how to use the X-ray along the d-file. 21.e4 is met with 21...♘xc3 22.♖xc3 ♖fc8 23.♘c6 ♕e8 24.♘xe7+ ♕xe7; the bishop is stronger than the knight, but black should hold with accurate defense. Petrovs chooses a different way and achieves his goal with incredible ease.

21.♘f5!?

Black could equalize easily with 21...♘xf4+! 22.♕xf4 ♕e8, but such a "Karpovian" maneuver did not fit the playing style of the young Kotov. He thought that he needed to make some tempo moves and get the rook into play.

21...♖fc8? 22.♗e5!

And it suddenly turns out that white has a lot of threats, and almost any reasonable move by black leads to material losses.

22...exf5. It was better to try 22...♕d8 23.♘xd5 exd5 (23...♘xd5

24.♖xd5 exd5 25.♕g4 ♗g5 26.♘e7+ ♕xe7 27.♖xc8+ ♖xc8 28.♕xc8+ ♕d8 29.♕xb7 loses immediately) – the position is poor, black has an isolated queen's pawn, but at least material is equal. After the game move, however, white simply converts his advantage.

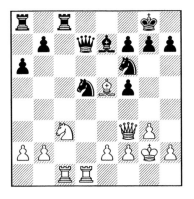

23.♗xf6 ♗xf6 24.♘xd5 ♕b5

24...♕e6   25.♘c7   loses   the exchange, so the author of the book *Think Like a Grandmaster* tried to give up some material in a more beneficial situation, but Petrovs was vigilant and cleanly transposed to a won rook endgame.

25.♖xc8+! ♖xc8 26.♕xf5 ♖e8 27.♘xf6+   gxf6   28.♕xb5   axb5 29.♔f3. Black is a pawn down, his pawn structure is in ruins, so the game didn't last long after that.

This   was   one   of   the   most discussed games of the first round – Alexander Kotov lost, and he could as well have resigned after 22 moves! Petrovs attracted a lot of attention from reporters, but, alas, he couldn't continue his winning streak.

Game 36
A. Konstantinopolsky – V. Petrovs
Moscow 1940, 12th Soviet
Championship, round 2
Caro-Kann Defense

1.e4 c6 2.♘c3 d5 3.♘f3 dxe4 4.♘xe4 ♘f6 5.♘xf6+ exf6 6.♗c4 ♗d6

Vladimirs   Mikhailovich   had already   played   this   line   at   the Buenos Aires Olympiad, the games were published in the Soviet chess bulletins, and so Konstantinopolsky followed   the   game   Michel   – Petrovs.

7.♕e2+

White doesn't try to refute the exf6 Caro-Kann – he just offers a queen trade that quickly leads to big simplifications and a draw. For instance, Petrovs once played 7... ♕e7 8.♕xe7+ ♔xe7 in Argentina, with a quick draw. However, after a brilliant win against Kotov, the leader of Latvian chess decided to try and build on his success...

7...♗e7   8.0-0   0-0   9.d4   ♗d6 10.♖e1 ♗g4 11.h3 ♗h5 12.g4 ♗g6 13.♘h4 ♘d7 14.♘xg6 hxg6 15.♕f3 g5

The   routine   15...♘b6   16.♗d3 ♗c7! 17.♗e3 ♕d6 with the idea ♘d5 and subsequent threat of a check on h2 was   completely   satisfactory,   but the opportunity to play ♘b6 won't disappear almost until the end. Alas, Petrovs was lulled by the peaceful check on move 7 and lost his sense of danger.

16.♔g2 g6 17.♖h1 ♔g7? It still wasn't too late to play 17...♘b6, but now Konstantinopolsky launches a decisive attack.

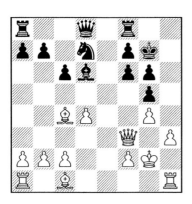

18.h4! gxh4

Now 18...♘b6 doesn't look too good due to 19.hxg5 fxg5 (19... ♘xc4 20.gxf6+) 20.♗b3 f6, but it at least saved black from an immediate disaster.

19.♗h6+! ♔xh6 20.♖xh4+ ♔g7 21.♖ah1

Threatening mate. Black is forced to give up his queen.

21...♖h8 22.♖xh8 ♕xh8 23.♖xh8 ♖xh8 24.♕b3, and white won easily.

This was a heavy blow, and the next few rounds were difficult for Petrovs. He was so distraught that he played poorly against Mikenas in round 3, lost a pawn but then managed to draw in the endgame with some precise defense. Then, in the game against Lvov master Isaak Gerstenfeld, Vladimirs Mikhailovich defended for all 40 moves and adjourned it with good

drawing chances. In the next round, he faced one of the two eventual winners of the 1940 championship, Andor Lilienthal.

Game 37
V. Petrovs – A. Lilienthal
Moscow 1940, 12th Soviet
Championship, round 5

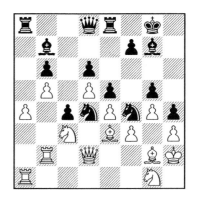

The black knights on f4 and d4 look very impressive, but the passivity of Lilienthal's bishops allows white to consolidate his defense. The simplest here was 26.♖aa2 ♘b3 27.♕f2, but Petrovs finds another, prettier continuation with an exchange sacrifice.

26.♗f1!? ♘b3 27.♕d1 ♘xa1 28.♕xa1

It turns out that black can't defend the c4 pawn due to the weakness of the b6 square, and Andor Arnoldovich gives it up to open the c-file and seize it with his major piece battery.

28...♖e7 29.♕a2 ♖c8 30.♖b4 ♘d3 31.♖xc4 ♖xc4 32.♕xc4 ♘f4 33.♕b3 ♕c7

Black has prepared to invade the opponent's camp, but an elegant knight pirouette prevents that.

34.♘a2! ♖e8 35.♘b4 ♖a8 36.♘c6. Draw. White's position is now impregnable.

Petrovs managed to score his second win in the play-off against Gerstenfeld – white was persistent in his will to win and went for a double-edged rook ending where Vladimirs showed his subtle endgame understanding yet again.

In round 6, the Latvian player had to face Mikhail Botvinnik. The Soviet champion had started his tourney with a surprise defeat from Igor Bondarevsky, who said afterwards in a private backstage conversation, "Botvinnik doesn't know how to play chess!" The Patriarch never forgave Bondarevsky for this phrase. Then, however, Mikhail Moiseevich subtly outplayed Boleslavsky and Levenfish and, like Petrovs, had 3 points out of 5.

I saw some claims that Botvinnik didn't prepare for this Soviet Championship at all – he was already dreaming about a match with Alekhine. This is, of course, untrue, as we can see from the games of this tournament. Before the event, the Soviet champion decided to learn to "serve with both hands" and studied 1.e4 openings extensively. Of course, Botvinnik used to play that move as well, but usually he used it against Caro-Kann players

(to get his favorite position with an isolated pawn in the Panov Attack) or against players who answered 1.e4 with some less sound openings such as Alekhine's Defense. Here, however, Mikhail Moiseevich crushed Konstantinopolsky and Rudakovsky in the Scheveningen Sicilian, subtly outplayed Veresov in the Four Knights Game (later, at the world championship match tournament, Botvinnik would defeat Reshevsky in the same line, showing that it's not that harmless) and broke through Petrovs' French bastions. It can be said that the move 1.e4 basically saved Botvinnik – without those 4/4 with white, they would probably have had to organize a 9-player round-robin tournament in 1941 rather than a 6-player one... Veresov, Dubinin and Makogonov finished just one point below Mikhail Moiseevich, who took sixth place.

Game 38
M. Botvinnik – V. Petrovs
Moscow 1940, 12th Soviet Championship, round 6

It was the first time that Botvinnik played 1.e4 in this tournament – he prepared well by studying Vladimirs' game against Gerstenfeld. Black hasn't got any counterplay on the queenside, and his position is very passive – the pieces are tied to defending weak squares. Still, his defense is solid, and after the tenacious 22...g6 23.h4 c4 24.♕c2 ♕c8 25.h5 (25.♘g5 ♖f6) 25...♕d8 26.hxg6 hxg6, the main battle is still ahead – the g6 pawn cannot be taken because this loses the g3 knight. In the actual game, black made a seemingly active bishop move, but overlooked his opponent's "jab".

22...♗f6? 23.f5! ♖e8

After 23...exf5 24.♘xf5, the white knight gets to d6; however, after the game move, white's dark-squared bishop activates immediately, causing Petrovs' position to crumble.

24.♗f4 c4 25.♕d2 ♘f8 26.♘e5 ♗xe5 27.♗xe5 ♕c8 28.♕g5

The black pieces are huddled on the last ranks, and the b6 and a5 pawns are meekly awaiting their fate.

28...exf5 29.♘xf5 ♘g6 30.♗xc7 ♖xe1 31.♖xe1 ♕xc7

31...♖xf5 32.♕d8+ ♕xd8 33.♗xd8 loses, but even with queens still on the board, it's not any easier for black.

32.♖e8+ ♖f8 33.♘e7+ ♔f7 34.♘xd5 ♕b7 35.♖e3 ♖b8 36.h4 ♔f8 37.h5 Black resigned.

Afterwards, Petrovs skillfully held a dangerous position against Bondarevsky, but the next three rounds were disastrous. In round 7, Vladimirs Mikhailovich adjourned a completely won position against Iosif Rudakovsky, with an extra exchange in the endgame. Rudakovsky finished dead last in the tournament, and, strictly speaking, didn't fit in with the distinguished ensemble of chess players all that well (even though Grandmasters Kotov and Levenfish took 18th and 19th place, which says something about the tournament strength – in recent years, both Alexander Alexandrovich and Grigory Yakovlevich had been among the leaders). However, Petrovs got into time trouble during the play-off, for some reason went for a position with a passed pawn race and barely managed to save the game as a result. And in the next two rounds, he had every chance to defeat the rising stars of Soviet chess, but completely crumbled close to time control.

Game 39

V. Petrovs – I. Boleslavsky
Moscow 1940, 12th Soviet Championship, round 9

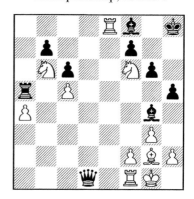

White has skillfully sacrificed his queen, and if he manages to coordinate his pieces, then a rook and two minor pieces will be stronger.

28...♕b3?

A mistake. Black should have tried to restrict the activity of the knight stuck on b6: 28...♕d4! 29.♘xg4 ♔g7 30.♘f6! ♕xf6 31.♖xf8 ♕e7 32.♖b8 ♖xc5 with good chances of saving the game.

29.♘xg4 ♔g7 30.♘d7?

An inaccuracy in return. 30.♘f6! ♔xf6 (30...♗xc5 31.♘bd7) 31.♖xf8 ♔g7 32.♖b8 ♖xc5 33.♖xb7 won immediately.

30...hxg4 31.♖xf8 ♕e6 32.♖d1 ♕e2?!

Both players were in time trouble, and Boleslavsky decided against the simple and strong 32...♖xa4 in favor of a cunning trap that Petrovs missed.

33.♖d4 ♕b2

white had a pleasant choice between 35.♖4xf7+ ♕xf7 36.♖xf7+ ♔xf7 37.♘e5+ ♔g7 38.♘xg4 ♖xc5 39.♗e4 ♖c4 40.f3 ♖xa4 41.h4 and 35.♗f1 ♖xa4 36.♖e8 ♖xf4 37.gxf4 ♕b4 38.♖e7 ♕xf4 39.♘e5, with significant winning chances in both cases.

34...♕d2!

White loses his knight! He could still fight for a draw with 35.♖d8! ♕e1+ 36.♗f1 ♕e7 37.♖b8 ♕xd7 38.♖c4, but Vladimirs instead gives up both the knight and two queenside pawns.

35.♖h4? ♕xd7 36.♖hh8 ♕d1+ 37.♗f1 ♖xc5 38.♖hg8+ ♔f6 39.♖d8 ♕xa4 40.♖d6+ ♔e7 41.♖gd8 ♖c1 42.♖8d7+ ♔f8 43.♔g2 ♕e4+ 44.f3 ♖c2+ 45.♖d2 ♖xd2+ 46.♖xd2 ♕b4 47.♖c2 c5 48.♖c4 ♕d2+ 49.♔h3 ♕f2 50.♗g2 b5 51.♖c1 c4 52.f4 ♕b2 White resigned.

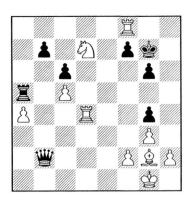

34.♖xg4??

The last step into the abyss. After 34.♖f4! ♕b3 (34...f5 35.♖e8),

Game 40

V. Smyslov – V. Petrovs

Moscow 1940, 12th Soviet Championship, round 10

In the next game, Petrovs played the Ruy Lopez as black instead of the French and confidently outplayed one of the greatest experts in the opening. We join the game with the white king very weak, which defines the evaluation of the position.

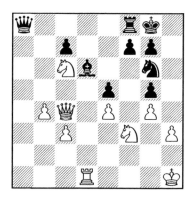

34...♛a4 35.♖d2?!

35.♖c1 prevented the black queen's incursion, but Smyslov, of course, decided against such a passive move.

35...♛a1+ 36.♔h2 ♛c1 37.b5?

White has to play very accurately so as not to lose immediately:

A drawing by the Soviet cartoonist Yuri Yuzepchuk, made during the 12th Soviet Championship. Like Petrovs, he would soon be arrested and perished in Stalin's Gulags

37.♔g3 ♖a8 38.♘a5. Now black could win a piece with 37...♘h4! 38.♖f2 ♛f4+, but adding the rook to the attack doesn't spoil the win yet.

37...♖a8? 38.♖f2 ♖a1 39.♘d8 ♛f4+ 40.♔g2

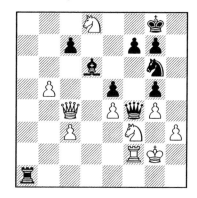

40...♝e7??

Black had just a few seconds on his clock, and Petrovs missed a simple blow that would have finished white off: 40...♝c5! 41.♛xc5 (or 41.♖f1 ♖xf1 42.♔xf1 ♛xe4) 41... ♛xe4 42.♔g3 ♛f4+ 43.♔g2 e4, crushing. Now the situation changes drastically, and it's Smyslov who lands a blow!

41.♘xf7! ♛xf7

And black's position is suddenly lost. 41...♔h7 42.♘3xg5+ was even worse.

42.♛xf7+ ♔xf7 43.♘xe5+ ♔e6 44.♘xg6

White has two extra pawns, and Smyslov, with his exquisite technique, won after the adjournment:

44...♝d6 45.♘f8+ ♔e7 46.♘h7! ♝f4 47.h4 ♖c1 48.♘xg5

♗xg5 49.hxg5 ♖xc3 50.g6 ♔e6
51.♖f7 ♖c5 52.♔g3 ♖xb5 53.♔f4
♖c5 54.♖xg7 ♔f6 55.♖g8 Black
resigned.

Had Vladimirs Mikhailovich not
missed his chances in these games, he
could have joined the leading group,
and the opposition he was to face in
the second half of the tournament
was somewhat weaker (except for
Keres)... But now Petrovs was on
a –2 score, and he faced an uphill
battle to escape the lower half of the
table.

Game 41
V. Petrovs – G. Levenfish
Moscow 1940, 12th Soviet
Championship, round 11
King's Indian Defense

1.d4 ♘f6 2.c4 d6 3.♘f3 ♘bd7
4.g3 e5 5.♗g2 g6 6.b3 exd4 7.♘xd4
♗g7 8.♗b2 0-0 9.♘c3 ♘c5 10.0-0
a5 11.a3 ♖e8 12.♕c2 c6 13.♖ab1
♘g4 14.♖bd1 ♕g5 15.b4 axb4
16.axb4 ♘a6 17.b5 ♘b4 18.♕b3 c5
19.♘f3

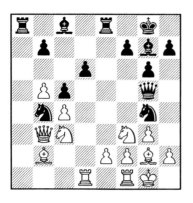

After the simple 19...♕e7 20.h3
♘f6, black would have had a good
position, but Levenfish decided to
set a trap and yet managed to walk
into it himself.

19...♕h5? 20.♖xd6 ♗f5 21.e4!
Black was probably hoping for
21.♖d2 ♗h6 22.h3 ♘e3 (still, even
this is much better for white), but
Petrovs' strong move refutes his
opponent's idea in the most simple
way.

21...♗xe4?
Black should have conceded the
pawn with 21...♗e6. Now the ex-
Soviet champion drops a piece.
22.♘xe4 ♖xe4 23.♗xg7 ♔xg7
24.♕c3+! ♔g8 25.h3 ♘h6

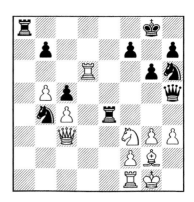

26.g4!
Black has to give up material to
save his queen. The remaining moves
were unnecessary.
26...♘xg4 27.hxg4 ♖xg4
28.♘e5 ♖f4 29.♘d7 ♕h4 30.♘f6+
♔f8 31.♘d5 ♖d4 32.♘xb4 ♖xd6
33.♕h8+ ♔e7 34.♕xa8 Black
resigned.

However, Petrovs couldn't return to the 50% level immediately: in round 12, he launched an overly enthusiastic attack against Petr Dubinin's queenside position, weakened his light squares and lost badly. Still, he didn't lose heart and scored two beautiful wins afterwards.

Game 42
V. Petrovs – G. Lisitsin
Moscow 1940, 12th Soviet Championship, round 13

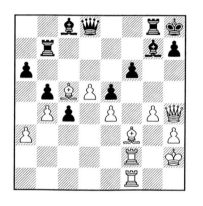

Petrovs had easily outplayed his opponent in the Old Indian Defense and now launches a decisive attack.

39.♗e2 ♗d7?

39...♖f7 would have forced white to find some precise moves, since neither 40.g5 fxg5 nor 40.♕g3 ♗h6 work. Now, however, an exchange sacrifice allows him to obtain a decisive advantage immediately.

40.♖xf6! ♗xf6 41.♖xf6 ♗e8 42.♗d6

The e5 pawn is lost by force, and the white bishop will reign supreme over the long diagonal.

42...♖bg7 43.♗xe5 ♗g6 44.♗f3 ♖e8

44...♕e7 45.♗c3 doesn't change the outcome; the game move, however, gave white an opportunity to execute a small combination.

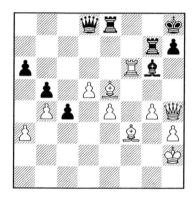

45.♖xg6! ♕xh4 46.♗xg7+ ♔g8 47.♗f6+ hxg6 48.♗xh4 c3 49.♗g5 c2 50.♗c1

Two bishops with pawns easily defeat the rook.

50...♖c8 51.e5 ♖c4 52.d6 ♖d4 53.♗c6 ♔f7 54.♗d7 Black resigned.

Petrovs faced young talented master Mark Stolberg from Rostov-on-Don in the next game. Mark sensationally took the lead in the first half of the championship, but crumbled after several unfortunate defeats and only finished 16th. In this game, Stolberg got unlucky, too.

Game 43
V. Petrovs – M. Stolberg
Moscow 1940, 12th Soviet
Championship, round 14

26...♔f8

Black avoids a possible threefold repetition after 26...♔h8 27.♘f7+ ♔g8 28.♘h6+. In his annotations, Petrovs wrote that he would have

continued the fight with 28.♕xg7+ ♔xg7 29.♘d6 ♗xe2 30.♖e1 ♗g4 31.cxb6 axb6 32.b5, but after 32... ♘c5! 33.bxc6 ♖ec8, black is alright. He could also play 30...♗d3!, preventing the queenside break and retaining the extra pawn.

27.♖d4! e5 28.♕d2!!

A beautiful resource! White pieces suddenly descend upon the black king.

28...♖ed8?

Allows an elegant finish. A more solid reply was 28...♖e6 29.♗h3! (white was counting on 29.♖xc4 dxc4 30.♕c3, with 30...b5 not working due to 31.♗xc6, but black had a very strong reply 30...♖ae8!) 29...♖ae8 (29...exd4 30.♗xe6) 30.♗xe6 ♖xe6 31.♕e3 ♔e8 32.♖d2 d4 33.♕a3, although it's very hard

Vladimirs Petrovs had a surprising ability to pick himself up and bounce back from setbacks

for black to defend this position with opposite-colored bishops.

29.♖xc4! dxc4 30.♕d6+ ♚e8 31.♗xc6 ♖ac8 32.♕e6+ ♚f8 33.♗e7+! The finishing blow. Black resigned due to inevitable mate.

Mark Stolberg's fate was also tragic and is detailed in Voronkov's book referred to earlier.

In the next game, Petrovs again played a Ruy Lopez – this time against Vyacheslav Ragozin. He slowly outwitted his opponent in a complicated rook endgame, but then got into time trouble again and threw away his advantage with a hasty 34th move. The Latvian champion drew with Vasily Panov but then suffered

an opening catastrophe in round 17 against Gavriil Veresov. Vladimirs was back to –1, but then managed to return to 50% again.

Game 44
V. Petrovs – V. Makogonov
Moscow 1940, 12th Soviet
Championship, round 18

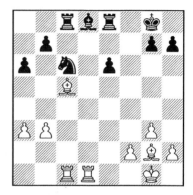

Erudite, always elegantly dressed and knowing several languages, Vladimirs Petrovs was constantly admired by his colleagues. Here with Smyslov, Keres, Rokhlin and Mikenas

Even such a renowned master of positional play as Vladimir Makogonov couldn't withstand Petrovs' Catalan Opening. White now has the bishop pair advantage, and black's pawn structure is weak. The Baku player needed to play 28... ♗f6, since the invasion on d7 is not a threat yet due to the pin along the c-file. Makogonov tries to exchange some pawns, but fails.

28...♘a5?! 29.♗e3 ♖xc1

There's no way back: 29...♘c6 30.♖d7.

30.♖xc1 b5

30...♘xb3 31.♖c8 ♔f7 32.♗xb7 a5 33.♗c6 ♖g8 34.♗a4 loses – the knight is trapped.

31.♖c8 ♔f8?

The last mistake. Black loses a pawn after 31...♔f7 32.♖a8 ♗e7 33.♖xa6 ♘xb3 34.♗c6 ♖b8 35.♗f4, but this loses the exchange.

32.b4! ♘c4 33.♗c6 Black resigned.

Before the last round, the standings were as follows: 1. Bondarevsky – 13.5, 2–3. Lilienthal, Smyslov – 12.5, 4. Boleslavsky – 11.5, 5. Keres – 11, 6. Botvinnik – 10.5, 7–8. Veresov, Makogonov – 10, 9. Dubinin – 9.5, 10. Petrovs – 9. Keres, who had white against Petrovs in the last round, had already lost his chances of a top-three finish and decided to treat the Moscow public to a King's Gambit. Paul Petrovich had only deployed it against weak Estonian players

before, but his success against Vladimirs then inspired him to play the old aggressive opening against grandmasters and masters as well. In the 1941 match tournament, Keres would crush Lilienthal in 19 moves, but in the German tournaments, the gambit wouldn't bring him any dividends: a draw against Schmidt, a loss against the little-known player Kubanek and a brutal rout by Alekhine. 8 years later, Keres would play 2.f4 against Vladimir Alatortsev, but a 33-move loss would convince him that the King's Gambit wasn't a good opening for him. The first outing, however, was rather positive.

Game 45
P. Keres – V. Petrovs
Moscow 1940, 12th Soviet Championship, round 19
King's Gambit

1.e4 e5 2.f4 d5 3.exd5 e4 4.d3 ♘f6 5.♘d2 exd3 6.♗xd3 ♕xd5 7.♘gf3 ♗c5 8.♕e2+ ♕e6 9.♘e5 0-0 10.♘e4 ♘xe4 11.♕xe4 g6

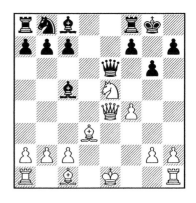

This position is characteristic of Keres – Petrovs games in general: Vladimirs relied on solid static positions, while Paul made sharp, dynamic moves, trying to create a whirlwind on the board.

12.b4!

Interestingly enough, almost all Soviet publications stated that this move was more or less the beginning of the decisive attack; however, black had a number of opportunities to maintain dynamic equality.

12...♗e7

Black could play 12...♗b6 13.♗b2 (not 13.c4 c5) 13...♘c6 14.0–0–0 (14.h4 is easily parried: 14...♘xe5 15.fxe5 ♕g4) 14...♘xe5 15.fxe5 ♕xa2 16.♗c4 ♗e3+ 17.♕xe3 ♕xc4 18.e6 ♕xe6 19.♕c3 f6 20.♕xc7 ♕f7, but the retreat to e7 is safer.

13.♗b2 ♗f6

The strongest move was 13...♘c6! 14.0–0–0 ♘xe5, and if white doesn't trade queens and instead goes for 15.fxe5?! ♕xa2! 16.h4 (16.♗c4 ♗g5+) 16...♗e6, then black just gets an extra pawn. With the bishop on f6, the white pawn will capture on e5 with tempo, but this is not a decisive mistake yet.

14.0–0–0 ♘c6 15.h4! h5?

Black could have played 15...♖e8 16.♖he1 (16.♗c4 ♕e7) 16...♘xe5 17.fxe5 ♗g7 18.♗c4 ♕f5, or even the dangerous 15...♕xa2! 16.♗c4 (not 16.h5 ♘xe5) 16...♗f5. Alas, such onslaughts by Keres always

got to Petrovs, and, in his attempt to play more solidly, he overlooked the pawn break that destroyed his defensive walls.

16.g4! **♗xe5 17.fxe5** **♕xg4 18.♕e3 ♘xb4**

Black is now two pawns up, but white sacrifices a third one, and then the white bishops just sweep away the remaining guards of the black monarch.

19.e6! **♘d5 20.exf7+** **♖xf7 21.♗c4 c6 22.♖xd5 ♕xc4 23.♕e8+** Black resigned. This game received the brilliancy prize.

Petrovs only took 10th place in the championship. On the one hand, this wasn't a complete failure, but, of course, he could have performed much better – Vladimirs Mikhailovich's actual strength, talent and contributions to chess were much closer to the top six players, who were later forced to play an additional match tournament because of backstage politics. Petrovs was greatly upset by missed opportunities in his games against Rudakovsky, Boleslavsky and Smyslov, and he named severe time trouble cases and lack of practice as the main reason for his relatively poor performance. Still, as a final tournament participant, he was directly seeded into the semi-final of the next Soviet Championship and could get a new chance to challenge the Soviet elite the following year

Alas, the situation in Latvia changed for the worse for the longtime leader of his small country. Petrovs wanted to take part in the reorganization of the Latvian Chess Union, but the new federation's top officials gave him the cold shoulder. Vladimirs' relationship with Alexander Koblenz, the young rising star of Riga and Mikhail Tal's future coach, was also strained.

In the socialist system, there was no such status as a "chess professional". Due to his poor relationship with the Latvian chess authorities, Petrovs couldn't get some sinecure as a chess coach or administrator, so he got a job in the Riga central registry office instead.

The first Latvian SSR Championship started soon, and Vladimirs Mikhailovich had to play there after work, as his wife put it, "as a second shift". The burden was immense, and Petrovs' start was catastrophic.

Game 46
Z. Solmanis – V. Petrovs
Riga 1940, 1ˢᵗ Latvian SSR
Championship, round 4
Four Knights Game

1.e4 e5 2.♘f3 ♘c6 3.♘c3 ♘f6 4.♗b5 a6 5.♗xc6 dxc6 6.♘xe5 ♘xe4 7.♘xe4 ♕d4 8.0-0 ♕xe5 9.d4 ♕f5 10.♖e1 ♗e6 11.♗g5 ♗d6 12.g4 ♕d5

White has a development advantage, but if black manages to castle, then the weakness of the g4 pawn will make itself felt. Solmanis now sets a cunning trap.

13.b3!?

13.f4 h6 gains nothing. The game move deprives the queen of the important c4 square.

13...b5?

The decisive mistake! After the precise 13...♗b4! 14.c4 (14.c3 ♗xc3!) 14...♕d7, black had great prospects. Now, however, he loses.

14.f4!

White threatens both to push the pawn further and to simply play ♘c3, trapping the queen.

14...0–0 15.f5!

Not going for 15.♘c3 ♗xg4 16.♘xd5 ♗xd1 17.♘e7+ ♗xe7 18.♗xe7 ♗g4 19.♗xf8 ♔xf8: white's position is technically won, but he still needs to convert his exchange. With an extra piece and an attack, however, Solmanis' task becomes much simpler.

15...♗xf5 16.gxf5 ♕xf5 17.♕d3, and white won easily.

Afterwards, Petrovs lost to Koblenz and made several draws... As his wife writes later in this book, "Petrovs came to the tournament straight from the registry office, where he worked as a deputy manager. Of course, nobody could expect great sporting achievements in such circumstances. Moreover, Volodya

Petrovs played Apsenieks many times, but only one photo of them playing together remains

himself treated this event as mere training, and when he finally pulled himself together, it was too late."

Vladimirs Mikhailovich made a desperate attempt to catch up with the leaders in the second half of the tournament, defeating Apsenieks, but this was only enough to share third place with Indulens (1. Koblenz – 13/17, 2. Apsenieks – 12.5, 3–4. Indulens, Petrovs – 12). Frustrated by this result, Vladimirs got down to business – he started working on analysis, preparing annotations to the games of the last Soviet Championship for Levenfish's book. Further, in early 1941, Latvian chess suffered a sad loss – maestro Fricis Apsenieks died from tuberculosis. The chair of the chief editor of the republic's main chess publication, *Atputa*, became vacant, and Petrovs, who had great experience as an article writer for various newspapers, including English ones, got the job.

That work was much more to Petrovs' liking! After his brief practice, Vladimirs began the Soviet Championship semi-final that started in summer 1941 in Rostov-on-Don in great form.

A lot of famous masters and promising youngsters converged on the shores of the Don (including David Bronstein, Alexander Tolush, Fyodor Duz-Khotimirsky and 14 participants of the previous championship) to determine the lucky eight who would join Bondarevsky, Lilienthal, Smyslov,

Keres, Boleslavsky, Botvinnik, Kotov and Levenfish in the next final.

The participants were divided into four groups, with the top 2 qualifying for the final. Petrovs' group included Chistiakov, Makogonov, Gerstenfeld, Kan, Khavin, Kirillov, Sokolsky, Tolush, Goldenov and Ravinsky. Vladimirs drew with Kirillov and Sokolsky at the start and then scored his first win.

Game 47
V. Petrovs – B. Goldenov
Rostov-on-Don 1941, Soviet Championship semi-final, round 3

Another opponent who couldn't withstand torture by the Catalan bishop. Its black counterpart is stuck on c8, and it's impossible to activate it without material losses.

22.♕a4 ♔h7?

Black should have tried to free the bishop at any cost: 22...♖xd1+ 23.♕xd1 e5 24.♕d5 ♗g4, retaining some chances. Now white goes for an easily won ending.

23.♖xd7 ♕xd7 24.♕xd7 ♗xd7 25.♗xb7 ♖b8 26.♗c7

The pawn onslaught decides matters.

26...♗e8 27.b4 ♔g6 28.♗a6 ♖a8 29.f4 ♔f6 30.♗d3 a6 31.♔f2 e5 32.fxe5+ ♔xe5 33.♖c5+ ♔d4 34.♖a5 ♔c3 35.b5 Black resigned.

Afterwards, Petrovs held a draw against Tolush, who played very well at the tournament, peacefully drew with Ravinsky and then scored his second win, against Chistiakov.

Game 48
A. Chistiakov – V. Petrovs
Rostov-on-Don 1941, Soviet Championship semi-final, round 3
Sicilian Defense

1.e4 c5 2.♘f3 ♘c6 3.d4 cxd4 4.♘xd4 ♘f6 5.♘c3 d6 6.♗g5 e6 7.♕d2 a6 8.♗e2 ♗e7 9.0-0 0-0 10.♘b3 b5 11.a3 ♗d7 12.♖ad1 ♕b6 13.♗xf6 ♗xf6 14.♕xd6 ♖fc8 15.♕c5 ♕xc5 16.♘xc5 ♗e8 17.♘b3 ♘e5

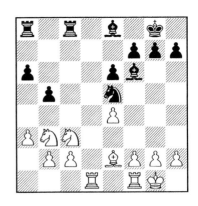

Petrovs has gone for a fight in the Rauzer Sicilian and has outwitted his opponent. Alexander Chistiakov ingenuously took the d6 pawn, but it seems that the bishop pair gives black more than enough compensation. White's only chance was 18.f4! ♘c4 19.♗xc4 bxc4 20.e5 cxb3 (or 20... ♗e7 21.♘d2 ♖ab8 22.♖b1) 21.exf6 bxc2 22.♖c1 gxf6 23.♖xc2 – the pawn is returned, but there's no bishop pair anymore. However, after

18.♖d6? ♘c4 white got crushed:
19.♗xc4 bxc4 20.♘d2 ♖ab8 21.♖b1

21.♘d1 ♗e5 22.♖xa6 ♗b5 23.♖a5 c3 also loses; the game move drops a piece.

21...♗e5! 22.♖xa6 ♗xc3 23.bxc3 ♖xb1+ 24.♘xb1 ♖d8! 25.♔f1 ♖d1+ 26.♔e2 ♖xb1 27.♖a8 ♔f8 28.♖c8 e5 29.a4 ♔e7 30.♖xc4 ♖a1 White resigned.

The standings after six rounds were as follows: 1. Tolush – 4.5/6, 2. Petrovs – 4/6, 3. Makogonov – 3.5/5, 4–5. Kirillov, Ravinsky – 3/6, 6–7. Goldenov, Kan – 2.5/5, 8–10. Sokolsky – 2/5, Chistiakov, Khavin – 2/6, 11. Gerstenfeld – 1/4 (the game Gerstenfeld – Kan remained unfinished). Vladimirs Petrovs had every chance of qualifying for the final – he was scheduled to play Gerstenfeld and Khavin at the finish, who had performed rather poorly. But then the Great Patriotic War started...

Petrovs attempted to get back to Latvia, but he wasn't allowed to go further than Abrene (currently Pytalovo, Russia) – Latvia had already been invaded by the Germans. At first, Petrovs served as a staff officer in the 201st Latvian Army; later he was recalled to Moscow to work for TASS, thanks to his foreign languages knowledge.

When the Third Reich army reached the outskirts of the Soviet capital, a famous city championship was held in Moscow (chess, despite the siege!), won by Master Isaak Mazel. Petrovs finished as runner-up, ahead of Panov and Alatortsev. In early 1942, a strong 8-player tournament was held in Moscow, featuring Moscow masters as well as Mikenas, Bondarevsky and Petrovs; the victory was mostly contested between the latter two. Igor Zakharovich finished half a point ahead, while Mikenas, Panov and Yudovich trailed 2.5 points behind.

Vladimirs Petrovs was in great form. Despite the privations of war, he had good conditions in which to study chess, communicate with other leading Soviet players, and absorb and process opening ideas... At that moment, he was, without a doubt, on the same level as the top six players of the 1940 Soviet Championship (and he would soon avenge his defeat against Boleslavsky!). But Petrovs never, even in his wildest dreams, could imagine that soon, three Moscow masters whom he trusted too much would write a denunciation against him...

In the meantime, Vladimirs Mikhailovich was evacuated to Sverdlovsk in the Ural Mountains; another chess tournament was to be held there. One year later, Botvinnik himself would take part in a Sverdlovsk tournament, but even in 1942, the line-up was impressive enough: Isaak Boleslavsky, Vyacheslav Ragozin, Vladimirs Petrovs, Vladas Mikenas, Georgy Bastrikov, Alexei Sokolsky, Abram Poliak, and Georgy Ilivitsky. In the first round, the Latvian player won the "Baltic derby".

Game 49

V. Mikenas – V. Petrovs

Sverdlovsk 1942, masters tournament, round 1

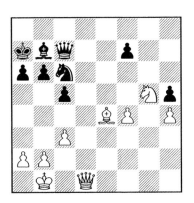

The position is roughly equal, and it seems that play should end with the mutual destruction of kingside pawns.

29...♕xf4 30.♕xh5

There was a more precise continuation: 30.♕f3! ♕xf3 31.♗xf3 f6 32.♘h7 ♘e7! 33.♗xb7 (33.♗xh5

♗e4+ loses a piece) 33...♔xb7 34.♘xf6 ♘f5 35.♘xh5 ♘xh4 with a draw.

30...f6 31.♕h7?

Now white loses a piece. He could have saved the game with 31.♗xc6! ♗xc6 32.♕f7+ ♗b7 33.♘e6 ♕xh4 34.♘d8 ♕e1+ 35.♔c2 ♕e2+ 36.♔c1, and the black queen cannot attack the white knight with check.

31...♕d6

Black threatens mate, and Mikenas loses the knight.

32.a3 fxg5 33.hxg5 ♕e7 34.♕f5 ♘d4 White resigned.

In the second round, Petrovs ground down Bastrikov in a long endgame, but then couldn't hold the ending against Ragozin.

Game 50

V. Ragozin – V. Petrovs

Sverdlovsk 1942, masters tournament, round 3

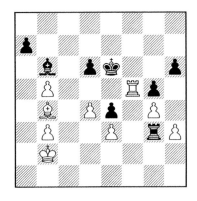

White has an extra doubled pawn, but black intends to capture the e3 and h3 pawns.

47.d5+ ♔e7?

Paradoxically, black could draw with the passive 47...♔d7! 48.♖f7+ ♔c8 49.♖f8+ ♔d7 50.♖f6 ♖xh3 51.♖xd6+ ♔c7 52.♖e6 ♖xe3 53.♖xh6 ♖d3 54.d6+ ♔d7, and he is saved by the passed e-pawn, while the d8 square is controlled by the b6 bishop.

48.♖e5+! ♔d7 49.♖xe4 ♗xe3 50.♖e6 ♗f4 51.♖xh6 ♖d3 52.♖h7+ ♔c8 53.♖xa7. After this, the white rook took down all black pawns, then Ragozin sent his king and b-pawn forward, winning after 74 moves.

Petrovs continued to chase the leaders – he crushed Sokolsky, then Poliak (the latter went for an incorrect combination). In the next round, he faced an illustrious opponent.

Game 51
V. Petrovs – I. Boleslavsky
Sverdlovsk 1942, masters
tournament, round 6

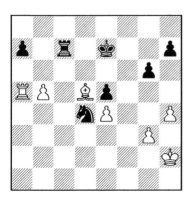

The hurricane of the King's Indian battle had subsided, and the endgame is roughly equal. Petrovs forces simplifications and sets a trap.

51.h5!? gxh5 52.♖a6

Now black could draw with 52...♘xb5 53.♖e6+ ♔f8 54.♖xe5, but Boleslavsky thought he could play for checkmate in the time scramble.

52...♖c2+ 53.♔h3 ♘f3

It was still not too late to capture the b5 pawn. Now white convincingly proves that the bishop is stronger than the knight on an open board.

54.♖xa7+ ♔d6

54...♔f6 55.♖f7+ loses a piece.

55.♖a6+ ♔d7 56.g4 h4 57.g5!

That's the trick! The white king escapes the mating net, and after 57...♘xg5+ 58.♔g4! ♖g2+ 59.♔xh4 ♘f3+ 60.♔h5 ♘d4 61.b6, black cannot hold the white passed pawn. Boleslavsky, unable to find any salvation, lost on time.

Petrovs was in second place with 5/6, just half a point behind Ragozin, but in round 7 Poltoranov scored a draw against him with white. The leader also made a draw (against Sokolsky), but soon the intrigue all but disappeared: Ragozin crushed Boleslavsky in 19 moves, while Petrovs lost to Vistaneckis out of the opening. Still, Vladimirs managed to edge out Sokolsky in the struggle for second place.

Game 52
V. Petrovs – G. Ilivitsky
Sverdlovsk 1942, masters
tournament, round 8

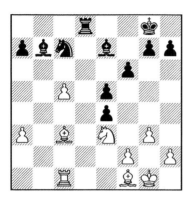

White has great compensation for the pawn, and after 27...♘e6 28.♗b4 ♗c6 29.♗c4 ♕f7 30.♘f5 g6 31.♘d6+ ♗xd6 32.cxd6, his chances are at least equal. Ilivitsky, however, didn't sense danger and blundered horribly.

27...♗c6? 28.♗a5 ♘e6

28...♖d7 is suddenly met with 29.♗h3. Black decides to give up the exchange in a different way, but Petrovs finishes the struggle with a series of energetic moves.

29.♗c4! ♕f7 30.♗xd8 ♗xd8 31.♘f5! g6 32.♘d6+ ♔e7 33.♘c8+ ♔d7 34.♗xe6+ Black resigned.

***

Vladimirs Petrovs was only 34 years old – just the age to challenge for the chess throne by the standards of the time. Considering his strong play and stable, good results, Petrovs could have probably performed very well in the first post-war Soviet Championship. In 1944, Boleslavsky took 3rd place, Makogonov and Mikenas 5th equal. I'm not sure if Vladimirs Mikhailovich could have competed with the top two, Botvinnik and Smyslov, but he certainly was not weaker than the next prizewinners – perhaps even stronger in some regards. Alas, this was not meant to happen, because very soon after the Sverdlovsk tournament, Petrovs was arrested...

There are still a lot of blank spots in Vladimirs Petrovs' story. Will we ever learn where he was buried? Or maybe some new facts that would shed light on the last months of his life? Meanwhile, we can only speculate how his fate would have worked out had he remained in the West after the Buenos Aires Olympiad, or heeded Flohr's warnings that it was better to keep silent in Soviet Russia because, as we know, the walls have ears. Looking at his last photo in freedom, depicting the wistful grandmaster, I play through Petrovs' games over and over again, placing the white king's bishop on the "sniper square" g2...

Part II: A Star Prematurely Extinguished,
by Galina Petrova-Matisa (2008)

The widow of Grandmaster Vladimirs Mikhailovich Petrovs remembers both the tragic fate of her husband and other family members crushed in the grinders of Stalin's repressions, but also the happy times of their short life together, including unforgettable meetings with the strongest chess players of the time.

"Shine, Shine, My Star…"

"If I die, then, over my grave, shine, shine my star." Did Vladimirs Mikhailovich Petrovs ever think that these words would be prophetic for him, that he would die in August 1943 in one of the camps of the Gulag Archipelago? He perished at the age of 35, at the peak of his physical and creative strength.

My husband loved the sentimental song "Shine, Shine, My Star". He often sang it, listened to it on the gramophone, and even played it on the piano. I remember him once saying to me, "Such beautiful, profound words." Maybe he experienced premonitions of his fate.

At my husband's request, I tried to find out who the author was, but during his lifetime I only managed to learn that the music was written by Petr Bulakhov, while the lyrics were anonymous – even though the authorship was attributed to Gumilev, Bunin and even Kolchak… Only much later did I learn that the real author of the lyrics was Vladimir Chuevsky, a law student of Moscow University. The song lingered in obscurity for many years and only became popular during World War I, thanks to the arrangement of the talented singer Vladimir Sabinin, who volunteered for the army. Sabinin made a true patriotic anthem out of the song, a declaration of love for the only true and coveted star – Russia. A record of Sabinin's version of the song was released in 1915, and the entire country started to sing it! And soon afterwards, the song shared the fate of many true masterpieces: it was mistakenly termed a "folk song". Petrovs had a notebook for recording quotes, thoughts, comments, and aphorisms of famous chess players. On the first page of this notebook, however, he jotted down this song's lyrics, which often baffled me. My husband never explained to me the relevance of those lyrics to chess.

Until his posthumous rehabilitation in March 1989, Petrovs' name was completely buried, struck out of chess life in both the USSR as a whole and Latvia in particular, even though he was the first Latvian grandmaster and represented the republic at all chess Olympiads and international tournaments. He didn't exist for his motherland. He was an enemy of the people.

Only abroad could you find articles about an "outstanding chess player", with his games printed and analyzed; chess players remembered their encounters with Petrovs and shared their guesses and speculation about his fate. Nobody knew anything, the man just disappeared without trace. They also asked me, but I knew nothing about my husband's fate either. Finally, after endless searches and appeals to the authorities, I learned that V. M. Petrovs was arrested in Moscow in August 1942, sentenced to 10 years of labor camp for anti-Soviet propaganda, and died while serving his sentence. *(According to Sergei Grodzensky in his book The Lubyanka Gambit, the author was told this information in 1948.)* There was nothing said about when, how or why my husband died. I spent decades trying to obtain this information. My requests for posthumous rehabilitation were refused several times. But it was necessary, and not only for me. I never lost hope that people would talk about Grandmaster Petrovs again and pay tribute to his chess talent, and that a star would once again shine over his grave – which is still unknown to this day. And indeed, after Petrovs' rehabilitation in 1989, his legacy has been gradually restored.

A New Passion That Became the Main One

Vladimirs Mikhailovich Petrovs was born on 27th September 1908 in Riga. An ethnic Russian, a Riga native. Petrovs' parents were also from Riga. His father was Mikhail Tikhonovich Petrov (Petrovs), born in 1872. His mother was Anastasia Parfenovna Petrova *nee* Grozdyakova. His father had a small cobbler's workshop on Avotu Street, with a modest shoe store. His mother was a housewife. They had three children: an older daughter Zinaida, a daughter Natalia and a son Vladimirs – the pride, joy and darling of the family. The Petrovs family rented a four-room flat on 64a Matisa Street, flat 4, not far from the workshop.

In 1919, Vladimirs Petrovs enrolled in the Russian middle school in Riga, unofficially known as the "Lomonosov Grammar School", since the building had hosted the Lomonosov Women's Grammar School until evacuation in 1915. Petrovs was a decent pupil, but only got especially good grades for the subjects that matched his interests – for instance, history, which later became a major hobby for him.

Petrovs' first passion was football. Nimble, quick, creative, able to use his head on the field, he was a natural-born footballer. Lomonosov Grammar was considered one of the strongest school teams in Latvia, and soon Vladimirs, despite stiff competition, became a forward for the school team. It was coached *pro bono* by the famous multiple-time Latvian football champion Redlihs. Vladimirs Berzins played for the team together with Petrovs. Both Vladimirs achieved good results in football. Later, Berzins chose football and became a multiple-time Latvian champion, while Petrovs found his calling in chess, though he never forgot his "first love" even after becoming a grandmaster.

If we believe the eyewitness accounts, Petrovs took up chess completely by chance, when he became bored of card games. One of the schoolboys' favorite pastimes was playing the local card game Zole. However, one fine evening, they decided against cards and found a board with pieces. Who knows – maybe, if not for this accident, we would have discussed a famous footballer instead. By the way, Petrovs was one of the best strikers in the football teams of the Union sports society and Rutenia student corporation[1].

By modern standards, Petrovs took up chess rather late, at the age of 13 (in 1921). Viktors von Rosenbergs taught the rules of the game to his classmates. And, as often happens, "the pupil soon surpassed the teacher", as Vladimirs captioned his first chess-related photo taken in 1923. Petrovs' friend Vladimirs Knohs remembered that after several "lessons", Petrovs challenged Rosenbergs to a "duel" of 100 games. The match went on for several months. At first, Petrovs lost one game after another, and the score was crushing in the teacher's favor. However, Petrovs managed to win the second half of the "duel" and the match itself, albeit with a minimal plus score. Even back then, Petrovs' ability to learn on the job was obvious.

April 1924 proved to be decisive in the 15 year-old boy's life. The range of Vladimirs' interests was quite wide back then. That year, Petrovs became the Latvian schoolboy football champion as a member of the Lomonosov Grammar team. It can be said that Vladimirs first traveled around Latvia as a footballer, and only later as a chess player. He also took up tennis at the time. But two circumstances practically "forced" him to choose chess as his life's work. First of all, he won the secondary tournament of the 1st Latvian Chess Congress and received a prize of 100 lats – this was a huge sum at the time, especially for a schoolboy. Vladimirs won his group convincingly, with a 100-percent score. He went through the final with no losses as well; for this, he earned first category and the right to challenge

---

1   Local university fraternities and sororities were known as "corporations" and a member was known as a "corporant" (male) or "corporantka" (female)

for the national master title at the 2nd Latvian Chess Congress. Still, the main reason for Petrovs taking up chess in earnest after the congress was Hermanis Matisons' prediction. Everyone knew that the first Latvian master was an unsurpassed endgame study composer and endings expert. As he handed Petrovs the prize for first place, he praised the endgame play in one of Petrovs' games and predicted a bright future for the young player – if, of course, he worked on chess seriously and thoroughly. And Matisons was notoriously stingy with praise.

Just three years after taking up the game, chess had become Petrovs' greatest passion. "The smell of the enemy's corpse is so pleasant!" the young Petrovs liked to say, referring to cases when his opponent was already losing, but hadn't realized it yet.

In 1925, Vladimirs graduated from school and got a place at the law school of Latvian University. From the start, he was active in the university's chess life. Studying chess took up a lot of time, so at first he visited the university as an unofficial student. Because of chess, it took him many years longer than normal to graduate from the law school.

Winners of the first Latvian Chess Tournament. A drawing by Sergejs Civinskis-Civis, published in the Segonya newspaper on 25 April 1924. Petrovs is portrayed as a baby. Civinskis-Civis was later executed by the Soviets

1926 was Vladimirs' stellar hour. He won the first Riga Championship and the Latvian Chess Club championship, becoming one of Latvia's strongest chess players.

That same year, he became an official student and retained that status for the next 15 years. Several circumstances were to blame for that. First of all, he traveled a lot to play in chess tournaments. Secondly, Petrovs' financial situation forced him to work in parallel with studies (he was a clerk in a train department, earning 70–80 lats per month). He also spent a whole year in obligatory military service, and, finally, he occasionally took medical leave to treat his lungs. It may sound incredible: such a robust fellow who loved active sports was ill with tuberculosis! But when

Petrovs was discharged from the army for health reasons in autumn 1937 – the tuberculosis process had become acute – very few people knew that this was the actual reason. Many thought that Petrovs had got an early discharge from the army because of his chess achievements.

The 4th Tournament of Nations (Prague 1931) became a turning point in the 22 year-old's career. He achieved the best individual result on board 3, and the foreign press finally took note of him. After the 2nd Olympiad at The Hague (1928), Petrovs' name was still obscure, but after the Hamburg Olympiad (1930), his name was mentioned among other promising young players. After Prague, if we draw parallels with the modern qualification system, Petrovs earned the international master title; however, to obtain the right to play in international tournaments that featured grandmasters, he needed to get some good results on at least second board.

After the 2nd Olympiad, Latvia took part in the next seven FIDE tournaments, and Petrovs played in all the subsequent pre-war competitions. At first, he had to go through qualification, but later, he was personally invited to play for the national team as one of Latvia's strongest players. Before the Warsaw 1935 Olympiad, the only question was which board he would play on.

At Hamburg, the players only learned the names of their opponents shortly before the next round. During Latvia's first three Olympiads, the line-ups for every match were chosen by the long-term team captain Fricis Apsenieks, the second Latvian master. In such conditions, he had to use all his tactical and diplomatic skills, because a poor line-up choice could lead to a lost match. In view of this, some tension mounted between Apsenieks and Petrovs. Before the match against France, the opponents' line-up was more or less known in advance: world champion Alexander Alekhine would always play first board at the Olympiads.

"...Many wanted to ask why Arvids Taube played against Alekhine, rather than Apsenieks or Petrovs? Petrovs wanted very much to play Alekhine, but the team captain deprived him of this rare opportunity, and, bafflingly, hadn't taken the opportunity himself either," the press wondered at the time.

The Latvia – France match (the last round of the Olympiad) ended in a 2–2 draw, with Alekhine, of course, winning his game. Petrovs took personal offense at Apsenieks' decision and, upon returning from the Olympiad, publicly criticized the Latvian team captain for poor choices numerous times. Apsenieks also didn't exactly mince words... The last sleepless night also played its role. Apsenieks miscalculated the amount of money needed, and our chess players had to spend the night before the last round

Petrovs as a corporant of Rutenia

on park benches. Later, Apsenieks presented this miscalculation as a funny curiosity. For three years, playing first board at the Olympiad was an impossible dream for Volodya.

However, there came a moment that helped Petrovs resolve this question once and for all – and it might be that he coldly planned everything in advance. After the first Latvian Championship in 1933, the champion was to be determined after a play-off match, since Apsenieks and Petrovs scored the same amount of points. Petrovs said to the press beforehand that he would not play such a match. As a result, the masters resolved the issue with a friendly compromise: Petrovs gives up the champion's title to Apsenieks, and in exchange, he gets to play first board for Latvia in all team competitions. Thus, Apsenieks got the champion's prize, honor and glory, while Petrovs made his dream come true – to play first board at the Olympiad! But this would only happen two years later, in Warsaw in 1935.

Lucky as Petka!

Friends considered Volodya a lucky man; he took pride in that and tested his luck at every opportunity. "Everyone is as lucky as he deserves," he liked to say. The future grandmaster's friends even came up with the adage, "Lucky as Petka!" He was nicknamed "Petka" (a derivative of his surname) to distinguish him from his namesake classmates – Vladimirs Svistunenko, Vladimirs Berzins and Vladimirs Germeirs (Knohs).

Now, turning page after page of the book of my life and evaluating everything that's connected with the Petrovs family, I come to the conclusion that they were affected by some kind of ill fate, which pushed me into the abyss together with them and messed up my life and the life of our daughter, Marina.

The fate of the entire Petrovs family was tragic... The older daughter, Zinaida, was married to a railway worker from Daugavpils, Garry Poleni. He died in 1929. There was an economic crisis in Latvia at the time. It was hard to get any work, and many went to Brazil to find some odd jobs – the country didn't require entry visas, and gradually a whole colony of Latvian citizens emerged there. Vladimirs' sister was among them. According to my husband, she was a very energetic, enterprising, practical and clever woman. Zinaida left her little daughter Tatiana in Riga with her parents, managed to start her own company in Brazil and had her parents and daughter transported there in 1932. Her life ended tragically and abruptly. Zinaida was killed with an axe by some young guy who tried to rob the cash register in her shop.

Their mother died in 1934. After an appendicitis operation, lights suddenly went out in the room, the doctor made some kind of mistake, and she died on the operating table. When I first met Petrovs, he still wore a mourning ribbon on his corporant's deckel[2]. In 1935, Vladimirs Mikhailovich, already a famous chess player, helped his father and niece get back to Riga; he also asked the government to transport the big car that belonged to his relatives to Latvia. This car was later used by his sister Natasha's (Natalia's) husband, who fell victim to Stalinist repressions and died in a prison in 1941 (the former White Army officer Fedor Schmidt).

Here is an extract from Vladimirs Petrovs' letter to his father and relatives in Brazil dated 21st September 1935, shortly before they came back to Riga:

---

2   A peaked cap worn by Latvian students

"I couldn't write anything long from Warsaw because I had no time – in addition to playing on first board, I was the Latvian team captain, with all the ensuing implications... Personally, I'm unhappy with the result, even though others are satisfied with the performance – both mine and our team's, which took 9th place out of 20. I won 7 games, drew 7 and lost 5. By the way, I defeated the South American champion, Grau, who is, undoubtedly, the strongest player of Argentina. Overall, I scored 10.5 points out of a possible 19, never managing to rest... To be honest, I'd hoped to score 14 or 15 points, that's why I'm unhappy. I unnecessarily lost a drawn game to Alekhine, and I shouldn't have lost to Flohr or the American, Fine, either – the latter even offered me a draw. In addition to these three, I also lost a clearly better position against Keres, the Estonian champion – by the way, he's a very young and talented player, just 19 years old. This was bad luck... Only Steiner from Hungary won a good game against me. I won my games without resorting to luck – that's good!

I returned from Warsaw on 2nd September. A beautiful city. We lived in the best district – at Aleje Ujazdowskie, with the amazing Palac Belwederski and a lot of green parks. Warsaw's main street, the Marszalkowska, was also in close proximity. We played in an official casino at the intersection of Ujazdowskie and Szucha. I might go to Finland for a tournament in October. Nothing has changed for the better at work. It's bad...

I want to graduate from university this year, to study seriously. Last week, Alekhine, the world champion, was a guest of honor in Riga. He gave simultaneous displays. I sort of worked as his "guide" and, of course, got rather tired. I also forgot to mention that in the last days in Warsaw, I caught a severe cold and even flu, which plagued me in Latvia as well. I played the last two games, against Tartakower and Austria's Grunfeld (I drew both), with a 38.4 Celsius fever. I would gladly go and meet you in Bordeaux, father, but I have no money. The visa and foreign passport alone cost about 40 lats. The trip to Warsaw also cost a lot of money, even though everything was paid in advance, and even the Latvian Chess Union gave me a 30-lat allowance, but I spent all of it..."

Once, after the war, when it was already known that Petrovs had been convicted, a Latvian chess magazine published an unflattering article that stated, among other things, that Petrovs was from a White Guard emigre family. This is blatantly untrue. Here's how the Soviet *Sahs [also known as Shakhmaty, Riga]* magazine described the alleged hopeless decline of chess life in pre-war Latvia:

"The masters felt no civil responsibility, they were only guided by the desire to keep their 'good reputation' so as not to lose their opponents in games for money stakes.

A prominent example of this is Master Petrovs' life. The son of Russian White emigres *(a familiar tactic – the Soviet press called Alekhine a "White Guard member" in 1940)*, well-educated, very talented and energetic, Petrovs could have become a strong personality and a prominent grandmaster in different circumstances. He understood the reasons for the decline of creative thought in the Western chess school, and so he studied the Soviet *Shakhmaty v SSSR* magazines extensively...

Starting with the unofficial match against the Austrian grandmaster Spielmann, Petrovs achieved many more successes in a short amount of time. All this got into his head, and his arrogance and egoism, which had manifested itself earlier, ran completely amok. Scandalous behavior, drinking, card games for money, a refusal to repay debts – Petrovs considered all this his privilege.

Petrovs' worldview was shaped by the 'best society' of bourgeois Latvia, which was hostile to the common people. Therefore, the establishment of Soviet rule in Latvia in 1940 was an unpleasant surprise for him."

Petrovs' friend and fellow student, Sergejs Karcevs, sent a rebuttal letter to the editor's office; they conducted some research and sent an unofficial apology for publishing false information. However, nobody bothered to publish a retraction. As I learned later, this article was written by the Latvian chess player Voldemars Mezgailis, who knew Petrovs very well. I don't know what he wanted to achieve with this slanderous article and who felt the need to publish it at all or why – it all remains a mystery to me.

Petrovs' father died tragically, all alone. By the time I returned to Riga with my daughter in 1945, after a long absence, my flat had been requisitioned by the Internal Affairs officers, and when I came to the Petrovs' flat, nobody answered the doorbell. The janitor helped me to open the door – and I almost lost consciousness because of the unbearable smell. A miserable, dying old man lay on the bed – he had literally been rotting alive because of gangrene in his leg. Nobody knew for how long he had been lying like that, all alone. He was immediately sent to the 1st city hospital. In the morning, when I ran to visit him, he was already dead. I was at a complete loss – I had no Soviet money, no Soviet passport, nothing. I didn't know whom to turn to, which of our friends were still in Riga. How to bury him? The hospital workers offered to bury him in a mass grave. I'm grateful to the janitor whom I knew for many years – he helped me sell some belongings of the Petrovs family and buy a coffin.

My daughter and I buried the old man: there was nobody to carry the coffin. I went outside the graveyard gate and asked three young men who were passing by to carry the coffin from the church to the grave. They apparently took pity on me and didn't even ask for money for their help. That's how the father of Grandmaster Vladimirs Petrovs was buried. His and Natasha's graves don't exist anymore. A highway was built over that part of the Pokrovskoe graveyard.

Petrovs' sister Natasha died during the German occupation, and in somewhat similar circumstances to her mother. She was getting discharged from the hospital after an appendicitis operation, and, as she was putting on clothes, she fell and died instantly due to a blood clot.

The Greatest Attack

Tracing the life of Grandmaster Petrovs and leafing through the pages of his biography which I started, I can't help but say that his fate was predicted by Finks, a psychic who was once well-known both in Riga and abroad. Before going to Argentina, my husband went to his photo studio to have a photo taken for *Atputa* magazine. As he was leaving, Finks told him that there was a photo in Petrovs' pocket, depicting a young woman with a child in her hands, and that he would lose her forever if he left on a long journey. Alas, Finks' prediction came true.

The second prediction was made by a Japanese astrologist on the steamship *Piriapolis* that brought the European chess players to the Olympiad in Argentina. He said, "Your star is shining bright, but it will fade soon!" Petrovs, of course, believed only the first part of the prediction.

Let this star shine bright forever, if only over his nameless grave...

I met my future husband in Hamburg, at the home of my uncle, Hermans Andreevich Punga, the Latvian consul at the time. I was a philology student at Latvia University and a member of the Russian female corporation Sororitas Tatiana. Petrovs, by then a law student, was already a well-known chess player and a corporant of Rutenia. *[Unfortunately, the author didn't indicate what year this was, but it appears to have been 1936.]*

I can't remember why Petrovs was in Hamburg at the time, and it's now impossible to determine. My first impression of him was of a cheerful, happy, easygoing man who could win anyone over. I liked his smile – it was kind and playful, baring his pretty white teeth. I was always jealous of his teeth and would later say that he smiled like that on purpose, to brag about them. When he smiled or laughed, small pretty wrinkles would appear on his nose (our daughter inherited them too, by the way).

Petrovs spent several days in Hamburg and went back to Riga, but I stayed. I received several letters from him; in one of them, he wrote that he gave a simultaneous display in Rezekne and visited my parents to get to know them.

Later, he confessed that he organized these simuls on purpose, to discuss me with them and, as he said with a laugh, to "put out feelers".

"You forgot that I am a chess player. All my moves are thoroughly prepared," he confessed. "The greatest attack in my life was my attack on you!"

As I returned to Riga to resume my studies, I started seeing Petrovs again. We met in the university, at the balls, at corporation events. Petrovs was a handsome man. Auburn, slightly wavy hair, big, gray, wide-spaced eyes, thick arched brows and long, upward-curling eyelashes. He was broad-shouldered and stocky, left an impression of a healthy, sturdy man. When he sat down, he looked like a tall, huge man. But it was not so. He was short in stature and was very anxious because of that, and, to be honest, I didn't like that at first. After we were married, he bemoaned his "unfortunate height" and he asked me to abandon my favorite high-heeled shoes.

Meeting him was always interesting. He was a great storyteller, especially in company. We all laughed heartily at his tall tales.

"Well, Petka, now that's obviously a lie," they would say, but he swore to God that everything he told was exactly as he said. Vladimirs was widely educated. Well-versed in literature, interested in history (he came to lectures together with me and loved to test my knowledge. I often failed these tests). He had an incredible memory. I remember revising for an exam in Egyptian history and couldn't remember all those countless pharaohs and their dynasties, but he, after reading the notes a few times, could recall any name, year, century and all those details which I couldn't memorize.

Petrovs was a musical man. I was learning the piano in the conservatoire at the time, so our interests were similar here as well. I was amazed at how quickly Petrovs could set up the chess board. "You could have played the piano well, you would have possessed good technique," I used to joke. Even though his hand wasn't exactly good for music: it was big and wide, his fingers were strong, thick and too short. I couldn't keep up with him in setting up the board. We even had this game – who could set up the board faster, and I always lost. And then he, laughing, asked me to show my technique on the piano. I only recently learned from the recollections of his school friends that he played in some orchestra at the dances, earning some money on the side. He never told me about that.

Volodya had beautiful, very clear handwriting – quite unlike my unreadable, jumpy one. He would often reprimand me after long and futile efforts to analyze my scrawl, "For God's sake, write more clearly – I have to look at your scribbling through a magnifying glass!" I remember once replying that I couldn't read what I had written myself. Volodya laughed, sincerely and gently. The newspapers wrote at the time that his handwriting remained steady even in difficult moments during chess games. "Graphology is not a required subject for chess players, but still, one can draw some conclusions based on handwriting. The hand of Latvia's third best chess player Petrovs never shakes, he doesn't get nervous, and even in the most critical moments, he writes down his moves with steady, almost calligraphic handwriting. The handwriting of many chess players suffers in difficult positions, and their characters are hard to figure out." Judging by handwriting, our personalities should have been the complete opposite. On the one hand, this was true, but, on the other hand, we had much in common as well: cheerfulness, a desire to connect with people, sociability.

Back then, life in Riga was in full swing. I mostly moved in circles of the Russian intelligentsia and students. We held Russian culture days and singing events. We were tightly connected with the Russian Drama Theater, which had a very impressive troupe back then (Vedrigskaya – "Vedrisochka", Melnikova, Bulatovs, Barabanovs, Yurovsky, Bungups, etc.). Famous artists came from abroad, including the Soviet Union. Together with Petrovs, I visited a Chaliapin recital in the Latvian University hall. We couldn't get to the other recital in the Opera, because the tickets were prohibitively expensive, and Chaliapin wouldn't give any complimentary tickets even to the conservatory students. We also visited the performances of Soviet artists: we saw Barsova, Sobinov, Mazhanova. Famous ballet dancers also came – Viktoria Kriger, Asaf Messer, Chabukiani, Vecheslova. We saw the famous Othello, Papazian, too. All in all, Riga was known as "Little Paris" at the time.

I remember the St. Tatiana Balls, held by Russian students, especially well. Student corporations played an active role in them. We, female corporants, were supposed to come in long white dresses and long kidskin gloves. The male students wore tuxedos and white gloves. The ball opened with a polonaise conducted by the famous dance teacher S. S. Vokhrameevs. With a monocle in his eye, wearing a tuxedo, very smart and elegant, he ran the show in impeccable French. Vohrameevs also fell victim to repressions and died in a labor camp.

I remember one such ball, with a photo surviving: Petrovs wearing a tuxedo, I'm wearing a white dress and holding a big balloon in my hands. These balloons became the reason for a quarrel with Volodya. The evening was ruined. I sold the balloons. The ball was both the main event of the academic year and the main source of money for the students' mutual assistance fund. Yes, before the war, all civic organizations performed charity work, including youth ones. The balls usually brought several hundred lats of profit. Thanks to this money, poorer students could get free lunches – the "Tatiana lunches", as they were known. The bulk of the money was used

We married in the Riga registry office in June 1937, and then we held a proper wedding ceremony that Christmas in Rezekne, my hometown

to pay for the education of those poor students.

I held huge bouquets made of balloons in both hands. Petrovs sided up to me (he was already a bit drunk), bought them all at once, donated a substantial sum (he probably borrowed some money to do that) and started to give the balloons away to everyone. This made me very angry for some reason. Holding the last remaining huge balloon in my hands, I told Vladimirs Mikhailovich that his showing off reminded me of antics of some drunk merchant. He took offense to that and tried to explain that there was no "showing off" in what he did and that I didn't understand him at all... We didn't make up at the ball, I went home, angry at Petrovs for ruining my evening.

We had such small quarrels all the time. Looking back now, it seems like naive childish jokes. "Misunderstandings" sometimes happened at the ice skating rink. In the very center of the city, at the so-called Esplanade, there was a skating rink. A live brass band played, pairs slid along the rink, and I liked to go there in the evenings. I was a decent skater and liked to dance on the ice. Petrovs sometimes went there, too. He was usually busy with chess in the evenings and was in great hurry, but it was difficult to take me away from the rink. I begged him to let me stay there, promising to follow him later. And then I once forgot to follow him... He lost the game and blamed me for that – which occasionally happened later as well.

Volodya could take offense easily, which led to more quarrels. Back when we were dating, my female student friends came up with an epigram and sang it at a student party in Volodya's presence.

Did you know that Galochka Zenets
Had a collection of hearts?
There's Kolya, there's Volodya,
And others like that!

I took it as an innocent joke and thought nothing about it, but Petrovs' face immediately changed, and he left quickly. He was incredibly angry at me, even though I had nothing to do with that. He couldn't forgive the words, "...and others like that." He thought that they were mocking him. What does "others like Petrovs" even mean? I remember telling him, "You've got delusions of grandeur, Vladimirs Mikhailovich!" We didn't speak for a while after that – I even decided to bite the bullet and swore to myself that everything was over. He liked to joke and laugh – but overreacted when he became a target for jokes himself, even the most harmless ones.

I'm very critical towards myself now. Of course, I wasn't a particularly good wife, but I loved Volodya very much, even though we squabbled a lot. He obviously loved me very much, too. He was very jealous. Jealous towards everyone and everything, even my parents' home. I often wanted to spend time there, I adored my mother and stepfather. Petrovs, however, always said, "Now your home is here. When a girl gets married, her parents' home should take a back seat."

At the St. Tatiana Ball

A Conflicted Person

I usually went to my parents' home in Rezekne during academic holidays and in summer. The house was big (11 rooms), there was more than enough space for everyone, and I invited student friends to stay with us. My parents always met me at the station with their four-legged family member – Lo, a beautiful Great Dane. My mom used to ask fearfully, "How many are there with you?" I usually avoided answering, and my mom silently counted how many people would follow me from the railcar.

Petrovs used to come too, of course. The Russian population of Rezekne still kept up the old patriarchal lifestyle. They followed old rituals and customs. They would go around with a star at Christmas, mummers came to our house, everyone was treated to cookies, nuts, sweets. It was noisy and funny, the dog barked at painted faces and masks, everyone sang and danced. Of course, nothing of the sort was happening in Riga by then.

On the Great Thursday of Holy Week, people carried burning candles home, trying not to extinguish them. It looked beautiful. Our Orthodox church was located on a hill, and multicolored lanterns dispersed in all directions – everyone was trying to bring fire to their home. And, of course, we went to church for the matins. My mom didn't give us any food beforehand; we broke fast later, then a priest came to us to bless the Easter table, and then the visits from the local intelligentsia started. My mother was the chairwoman of the Pushkin Society, took part in Russian cultural life, and so she had a lot of acquaintances. She paid for that with a 16-year exile…

The sweet, faraway past. Happy youth. Petrovs loved to come to my parents' home on these holidays, and then unhappily went back to work. I had no job, so I could stay for longer.

They say that the past always looks beautiful. I'm not idealizing it – I'm just describing the atmosphere that surrounded me and Petrovs at the time. Of course, there was also another life around us. There were the jobless, the underground, people were jailed, they fought for their ideas, they were unhappy with the political system. All this did happen, but I cannot say anything about it – I never encountered this "other life" directly, because both I and my social circle were far removed from politics. Petrovs was also apolitical – so I can't really comprehend what happened and what led to his death.

Now, more than half a century later, it's hard for me to write about the past. It's also hard for an elderly woman who lived a difficult life to objectively evaluate the people and events of long ago. Even my own husband. I'm not Galka anymore – the young woman who played a significant role in

In my corporation I was the Magister-Cantandi ("Mistress of Song"), but I had a simpler nickname – the "song-bird dance-fly"

V. M. Petrovs' life, who shared his short life journey with him. I'm looking at her as a complete stranger, and I'm not surprised that she couldn't understand Petrovs in many ways. It seems that his acquaintances and even closest friends couldn't understand his essence either. As I re-read Petrovs' letters to me and some of mine to him, which I found in his table during the German occupation (he was already dead at that point), bound with a ribbon, I came to the conclusion that he was a true romantic! Even though he always thought that *I* was a romantic. He could have probably written an entire treatise on the phenomenon of love. Of course, Petrovs was a very conflicted person, which showed in everything: romantic on the one hand, but a sober, practical realist on the other. How could these two traits coexist within him? I couldn't understand it back then, and I think that I couldn't really figure him out and understand him in the four and half years that we lived together.

Do we even need to figure him out now? Why? The important thing that he *was*, that he was in my life, that he left a bright trace, and my life with him, no matter what happened, now seems the happiest time in all my life.

I'm amazed why I still remember all that in the smallest details – I completely forgot many other things. I think that this was my ultimate mission – to wait for a time which demands that I rescue the honorable name of Vladimirs Mikhailovich Petrovs from the abyss of oblivion, injustice, brutality and lawlessness.

I remember – and many people who knew me back then also confirm – that I was a joyful, fun, life-loving person. I had a lot of friends, and, as Petrovs would say later, I couldn't live without people. I loved to laugh and joke, and I was the *Magister Cantandi* ("Mistress of Song") of my corporation – they called me the "song-bird dance-fly". My mom once said that I would get premature wrinkles around my mouth from all that laughing. And I told her, "Mommy, I'm so grateful to you. My life is so wonderful!" My sweet, good, kind mother! You were right: I did get premature wrinkles, but, alas, not from laughing, but from all the paths I had to tread, and my hair turned salt-and-pepper color too early, too. My mother, who returned years later from the faraway North with a disability, my beloved and once beautiful mother, reminded me of my words.

My First Encounter with Chess Players – Paul Keres

I was interested in many things back then; the only thing that left me completely indifferent and disinterested was chess. Later, I regretted that, and constantly reproached myself after losing Volodya. But all that happened much, much later. As they say, "We don't keep what we have, and we cry when we lose it." For Petrovs, chess was an integral part of his life, he probably wouldn't have been able to live without it, whereas I didn't even bother to try to understand this ancient game. Volodya did try to rouse my interest several times, he would explain everything to me very thoroughly and patiently for ages, but he finally gave up, seeing that this was truly hopeless, and chess was "not for me". He upset me greatly when he said that I couldn't think logically at all; I got angry and showed a 5 *[the highest grade in the Russian education system]* for logic in my gradebook. Petrovs was surprised and said that my professor didn't know the first thing about his own students. Yet another quarrel with my dear and infinitely beloved Volodya.

Petrovs adored chess. To all intents and purposes, it was his life. "I enjoy playing chess. The thought that I need to score points, even half a point, immediately kills any creativity within me. It's like when you look at some work of art that you want to purchase and suddenly forget about the work itself and start counting money."

I asked him many times what drove him the most in chess? Simply playing, the will to win, the actual struggle, or a desire to prove himself, to become the best, the number one? "And what is music for you? Why do you play it? Why do you take part in concerts and competitions?" he would answer, posing a question of his own. I finally found an answer that was common for both of us: "self-expression".

In June-July 1937, a big international chess tournament was held in Kemeri. We were already officially engaged back then. Customs demanded that we inform everyone in our corporation about our engagement with a postcard. I kept one of those postcards. It had the colors of Volodya's corporation on

After his first trip to Moscow, Volodya said to me, "I went to the bath-house. The attendant was beating the air with the sauna whisk, and he said to me: 'Sir, you are clearly not local. Where are you from?' I was surprised. I enquired as to why he thought that I wasn't local. 'Because nobody here wears a crucifix, all the more so in public...'" Volodya then told me, "I hadn't even thought of that. Well, I'm not going to hide my crucifix, even in the bath-house"

one side, and my own colors, green, blue and red, on the other side. (These colors symbolized truth, goodness and beauty: the motto of Sororitas Tatiana was "For Truth, Culture and Unity".) In addition, the fiancee had to give a *Bierzipfel* to the fiance as a gift. This was a wide leather ribbon for a pocket watch, with a pendant painted in the colors of the Rutenia corporation, white, orange and black. The fiance gave the fiancee a brooch painted in the colors of the women's corporation.

Petrovs arrived at the Kemeri tournament straight from his military unit – he was carrying out military service at the time, so he sported a buzz cut. Of course, this didn't do any favors for his appearance, he was nervous and upset and begged me to come as soon as possible. I had to console him and tell him that he still looked good. I could only come after my exam session was over. Thus, I missed the impressive opening ceremony and the first four rounds. Petrovs gradually introduced me to all the tournament participants. I was at a loss at first. Since I was far removed from chess life, I didn't know anyone, and had only heard some of their names.

I'm easygoing with people – this was one of the things I had in common with my husband. However, he was stricter in his assessment of people, kept his distance and didn't pour his heart out. I reproached him, saying that he was too quick in labeling and evaluating people without even knowing them all that well. On the other hand, I, according to him, was too trusting, and I would see how treacherous and disingenuous people can be in the future. He was right in many ways.

I immediately liked Paul Keres when we met. A modest, tall and lean young man, with a clever, serious, intelligent face. I thought that he was likable, and I said as much to Petrovs; he also spoke of Keres with warmth, saying that he was

A Bierzipfel

very talented and had a bright future, and that he always feared facing Keres at the board. Keres was almost the same age as me, we were both students. Paul studied mathematics in Estonia. He spent all his free time at the tournament with another young man – his secretary, who was almost always at his side.

I got to know Keres more closely in the following way: Petrovs was analyzing an adjourned game, and I brought a book and went to a park located right behind the hotel. This was a splendid, huge park adjacent to a dense forest. As I walked around, I stumbled upon Keres' secretary, who was anxiously looking for him everywhere. I told him that I hadn't seen Keres, and he turned a corner to some side alley; I walked on and, entering the thick of the wood, suddenly saw Keres in a secluded place, sitting on a bench. He seemed to be hiding from everyone. I told him about meeting his secretary, and he smiled kindly and asked not to reveal his location – he wanted to spend some time alone. I was heading off, but he asked me to sit down and talk a bit about anything but chess. When he learned that I knew nothing about chess and the life of chess players and never read chess magazines, Keres seemed to be relieved. He said that this was good for me, but then it's a surprise that I chose a chess player, of all people, as a husband. I said that opposites probably attract...

Keres said that Petrovs was a talented and promising chess player. We discussed life in Latvia and Estonia, our universities; Keres complained that he had no time for studies and said he feared that chess-related travels would prevent him from finishing his education altogether. That's how we became acquaintances and then friends, and I gratefully remember his respect for me and sincere concern and compassion later, because of Petrovs' tragic fate. He was completely sure of his innocence; Keres was virtually the only chess player who honored my husband's memory and didn't turn away from me. I honestly don't know what was stopping others from doing the same. Fear? Fear to mention a repressed man's name years and even decades after his death?

At the tournament, I also took notice of an elegant, beautiful young woman in tasteful clothes. This was the wife of the famous chess player Salo Flohr, Raisa. She was always accompanied by a small white dog called Berry. "Raisa looks like Chekhov's Lady with the Dog," I once said to Petrovs. He laughed, and we always called her "Lady with the Dog" afterwards in our conversations. We quickly got to know her, and we were inseparable by the end of the tournament. She called me "Galyusha", and, like Keres' secretary, would look for me everywhere, drawing Petrovs' ire and even something akin to jealousy.

The Lady with the Dog – Raisa Flohr

Both Raisa and I wanted to natter, share gossip, discuss clothes and basically anything not involving the wins, losses and adjourned games of our husbands. Raisa had a lot of expensive and beautiful clothes and jewelry, and her shoe supply seemed endless. I wasn't spoiled in that regard – I was just a young student, used next to no cosmetics, and had a smooth, boyish haircut. Of course, I liked to look at Raisa's clothes and ask for her advice on cosmetics, which she had in abundance. She had a complicated machine for eyelash curling; I tried to use it once and it pinched my eyelid so painfully that the eyelid reddened for ages, and I almost ended up cross-eyed.

Raisa's comments about my nose got to me so much that several years later I nearly got a nose job in Paris. It's lucky that Volodya categorically refused to pay for it

On another occasion, she wanted to gift me long, prominent earrings with blue jewels, which supposedly suited me very well. Of course I declined, even though Raisa assured me that I had to wear something long on my ears, because this contrasted with and lengthened my round face and snub nose. I bought similar earrings in Prague later, but Volodya disapproved and

On the terrace of our Kemeri hotel during the decisive game with Flohr

said that they didn't suit me at all, and I shouldn't lengthen my round face and snub nose. In Kemeri, Raisa tried to conceptualize and draw my future wedding dress several times. I kept her "designs" for ages, but never actually used them – they were too complicated.

I often sat with Raisa in a cafe located on the huge hotel terrace; the tournament hall was nearby, behind a glass wall. I have two photos in my album: Petrovs playing Flohr in one, and me drinking coffee with Raisa in the other, with a caption written by Petrovs, "…but they're thinking of other things." I'm sure that both of us wanted our husbands to win. Raisa understood chess well enough and was surprised by my indifference. I felt awkward and made an excuse that I wasn't interested just yet, but that I was studying the game.

Raisa told me a lot about herself. She was a movie actress and had lived in Moscow (her maiden name was Kristalinskaya), but now she lived in Prague with her husband; she liked the city, but still missed Moscow (Salo didn't want to move there). She praised life in Moscow – everything was good in the Soviet Union, life was interesting, no shortages of anything. However, she never once said that all her pretty clothes were bought abroad. Back then, I believed everything I was told, and there was chaos in my thoughts after hearing her information about the Soviet Union.

The Flohr couple loved their dog Berry. Raisa said that the Moscow security organs recommended that they rename her. When I asked why, she hinted vaguely that this name sounded similar to Beria. (I didn't even know who or what Beria was back then, and didn't ask further questions.) That's how Berry became Mary. But when they got to England, they renamed the dog yet again, Terry, because they thought that it was embarrassing to have a dog that shared a name with the English queen.

Even though Raisa and I became good friends – at least, I thought so – Petrovs clearly disliked her, thinking that she was shallow, but possessed a good imagination. He didn't believe that her friendly attitude towards me was sincere. "Believe me, you'll see it for yourself, eventually." Perhaps he was right even back then, but I only saw the proof of his words after the war, when I learned that my husband was arrested. I knew nothing more about him. I wrote several letters to the Flohrs – they had already moved to the Soviet Union, fearing genocide from the Nazis – begging them to tell me anything they knew about my husband's fate. I hoped that my friends would invite me to Moscow and help me with my search. I begged them to reply. Even the Vorkutlag chief, whom I also contacted, did send a reply to me and didn't just throw my letter away.

How naive I was! Of course, I received no reply from Raisa. I was very bitter – I still believed in friendship. Then I remembered Volodya's words. Now I'm not surprised at anything anymore, though I won't say that I understand – I don't

Still, back in that faraway time, my relationship with the Flohrs was very warm. Salo was also very likable. I can't say that it was friendship, but our conversations were always very pleasant. His kind attitude towards me was definitely sincere. He was a simple man, I saw no conceit or arrogance in him, even though he was already famous. The Czechs loved him dearly and were proud of him. I was sure that he was a Czech, and only much later did I learn that he was Jewish – Salomon Flohr. Raisa was Jewish, too, even though she told me that she was Russian.

In the evenings, we would go for walks in the Kemeri parks, talking a lot. Raisa, of course, spoke perfect Russian, while Salo talked with a heavy and incredibly cute accent. Sometimes Landau joined us – he was probably a friend of theirs. Landau was a huge, portly man, and we all looked tiny in comparison with him. A big photo survived: the Flohrs, Landau, Petrovs and, of course, Berry. Salo loved his dog, always took it to the tournaments and considered it his mascot; Petrovs once said to him, "You have a canine mascot, and I have an avian mascot – Galchonok[3]." Afterwards, Salo would always

---

3   The name Galka (a diminutive of Galina) is also the Russian word for "jackdaw"

call me "ptichka" ("birdie" in Russian), pronouncing it with a heavy accent, more like "ptyshka".

I loved Flohr's smile. It was childish, gentle and sweet. His laughter was often infectious – he was similar to Petrovs in this regard. During the second Kemeri tournament, in 1939, the Flohrs visited us several times. Salo would pick up our daughter Marina and play with her, he seemed to love children (they didn't have any kids of their own). Petrovs took some photos, but only one survived – Salo holding the little Marina. Volodya loved his daughter and photographed her endlessly. Admittedly, he wanted a son. I promised him a son providing he gave up chess. I often tried to persuade him to do this. I said we would live a quiet life, without stress. So he promised. I wonder, had life turned out differently, whether he would have kept his promise. Now, at the end of my life, this all seems like harmless joking.

I remember a funny story from that period. I invited over the Finnish chess player Book together with the Flohrs. He was above average height, stocky, calm, fair-haired, a bright-eyed Finn. A typical Norseman. My daughter wasn't in particularly good health – there was something wrong with her stomach, and he gave me some advice (he probably had a small child of his own, since he was well-versed in the matter). My husband and I were working in the kitchen, Salo held Marina on his lap, Raisa set up the table, and Book sat in a chair. I heard my daughter crying – apparently, she wet herself. I put her on Book's lap and went to another room for some fresh clothes. When I picked her up, I was horrified to see a huge wet patch on his light-colored trousers. He sat there, shy and flustered, and I was desperate, almost cried and apologized profusely before him. I can't remember Flohr laughing so loudly ever again. Of course, my husband reprimanded me

The Flohrs' dog was called Berry, Mary and Terry!

for my rash actions. Both chess player guests defended me, Salo even said that this was a "lucky sign", and Book would surely win his difficult game tomorrow. The next day, my husband told me that poor Book had been forced to take his trousers for an emergency clean, his game was adjourned in a won position, and he indeed did win it the day after that. I was so happy! Flohr would later joke that I should repeat the same "experiment" before Petrovs' difficult games.

We also visited the Flohrs in Prague. There were no international tournaments in Prague at the time, but Petrovs had several simultaneous displays booked. The Flohrs lived in the city center. They had a big room, a sort of studio flat, very tastefully furnished. Raisa had great taste overall. She watched over her husband's appearance; Salo was always dressed elegantly, with well-chosen ties, shirts and shoes. Without a doubt, we should credit Raisa for that. We would walk around the city together a lot. They showed us some landmarks, took us to picturesque places in the countryside. Petrovs had visited Czechoslovakia before, it wasn't new to him, but I was enraptured by the beautiful "Golden Prague".

We once discussed Moscow in Flohr's apartment. Remembering all the things Raisa told me about the Soviet Union in Kemeri, I asked Salo, without any ulterior motives, why he didn't want to move. Raisa desperately wanted to return, and no matter how good Prague was, she missed her hometown.

Visiting the Flohrs in Prague, 1938

Salo suddenly answered very harshly, which was uncharacteristic for him. His opinion about life in the Soviet Union was the complete opposite to Raisa's, which was unexpected for me. He said that you had to fear for your every word there, that everyone was eavesdropping, that you always had to keep in mind that someone would denounce you. Every new person, especially if they come from abroad, was being watched. Raisa disagreed and argued with him. I felt that this made her uncomfortable. She couldn't forget everything she told me before, could she? Salo's answers became more and more exasperated...

So I accidentally caused a row between them. I'd never seen Salo like that nor heard such things from him. That evening, I realized that not everything in their life was so idyllic and smooth. It would be interesting for me to know what Salo was like and how his outlook changed after he moved to the Soviet Union and became its citizen. I only recently learned that he divorced Raisa and married another woman, and the news of his death saddened me.

I also met the chess player Karel Opocensky in Prague. I thought he was well-disposed towards us. At any rate, he was very attentive and helpful there. My Uncle Vanya was buried in Prague – my mother's brother, who had a Czech wife. He was a famous aviator, called "King of the Air" in Czechoslovakia. In the early 1930s, he crashed while performing some trick (I think it was a loop-de-loop). There was a splendid funeral that my mother attended. The state funded the funeral and erected a beautiful monument to him. My mom brought back a piece of the wing of the plane Uncle Vanya crashed in, with his photo embedded in it. Karel helped me find the cemetery and went there together with us. He spoke very warmly of Petrovs. So just how could he have said that they don't imprison you for nothing after Volodya was arrested?

We met the Flohrs several times later, in Stockholm. Of course, there was no such talk anymore, and nothing changed in our relationship. We never thought that the Baden tournament would be the last time I'd ever meet them. Volodya did meet them later, in the Soviet Union. I don't know what kind of relationship they enjoyed there, or whether they met outside tournaments. I only know that Flohr died, and I haven't tried to find Raisa.

A Hero for All Life – Alexander Alekhine

Let's get back to meetings and acquaintances at the Kemeri tournament. Petrovs, of course, was the one who introduced me to the Alekhines. I was very shy before Alexander Alexandrovich, feeling like a little girl. He was tall and well built, with fair hair. Small eyes, either gray or blue, which seemed expressionless to me – probably because of his nearsightedness. He spoke little. I didn't see him mingle with anybody during the tournament. Petrovs told me a lot about him. He said that when he was 17, he heard that Alekhine set a record in Paris in 1925, giving a 28-board blindfold simultaneous display; he was flabbergasted, and Alekhine became his hero for all his life. When I reproached Volodya for excessive drinking, he would say that Alekhine played his most beautiful games "under the influence". I don't know whether it's true, but I remember Volodya's words.

Alekhine seemed rude and sharp-tongued to me, and I soon realized that I simply feared him. A close friend once came to visit me, and we happened to meet Alekhine and his wife. "He's so unpleasant," she later said, but she adored Salo Flohr. I didn't like Alekhine's wife either – I met her in Kemeri and then in Margate. During her husband's games, she usually chose a comfortable place with a good view and knitted, watching him play. Her first question to me was whether I could knit – every woman should be able to! I was expecting a child at the time, and she pestered me endlessly: you walk too fast, your heels are too high, you don't dress according to the weather, etc. I remember climbing on a windowsill in my hotel room to straighten the curtains. She entered the room as I did that (they lived in an adjacent

The day before the Kemeri tournament began. June 1937

room), got horrified and chastised me as though I was a small child. I don't remember the exact words or even language (not English – I spoke it poorly, maybe in German), but I do remember that I was offended. Petrovs would later ask me what I did to cause such an outburst from her, why she called me careless and reckless. I answered that it was just a windowsill... I don't think he understood exactly what had happened. This was my last meeting and failed contact with Mrs. Alekhine.

When I asked Alekhine whether he wanted to go back to Russia, he answered, "NEVER!" The only things he remembered in the Soviet Union were famine, poverty and devastation. I was rather disappointed when I saw the movie *Russia's White Snow* about Alekhine's emigration. Salo Flohr didn't look like himself at all (neither in appearance nor in personality), Alekhine's wife didn't either, and where did they get Alexander Alexandrovich's homesickness from?! He answered my second question, "Do you have relatives left there?" and he answered "No." Now I know why he said that. I lived through that myself... Only much later I learned that he had a brother, Alexei, and a sister, Varvara, who both officially disowned Alexander Alexandrovich for his anti-Soviet views.

I remember Alekhine getting back at the younger players who made jokes about him in Kemeri in 1937. Before his game against Volodya, Alekhine approached the tournament board when both Flohr and Reshevsky stood there. He took the chalk and nonchalantly wrote half-points for himself and Petrovs in the table. Flohr and Reshevsky were indignant – prearranged draws violated the gentlemanly code of honor. Alekhine's answer, why couldn't he gift half a point to Petrovs, caused even more indignation from the tournament leaders. And then, Alekhine upped the ante: he erased the half-points and wrote a zero for himself and a full point for Petrovs...

Petrovs surprised the whole chess world in Kemeri that year, sharing first place with Grandmaster Flohr and the American former wonderkid Reshevsky. By the way, according to Volodya, the tournament was the fiercest of all the tournaments held in Europe in the last four years.

His shared win surprised the participants and spectators alike, and seemingly even Vladimirs himself. By request of the other winners, Reshevsky and Flohr, the first place prize, a gift from Karlis Ulmanis, the president of Latvia – a folk-style box with carved chess pieces and an amber-encrusted chess board – was presented to Petrovs. However, Petrovs had to pay compensation for it. The first three prizes, 1,000, 750 and 500 lats, were divided equally between the winners. And Book received a special prize (50 lats) for "the game that decided the outcome of the tournament".

By the unofficial rules of the chess world at the time, if six grandmasters took part in an international tournament, the winner also received the grandmaster title. Since the Kemeri tournament featured seven grandmasters, Petrovs also received this unofficial title. Both the Latvian (since 1937) and international press (especially in articles on the Buenos Aires 1939 Olympiad) started calling Petrovs a grandmaster. The Soviet Union obviously didn't recognize his title. Still, Petrovs was one of the few Latvian players who received the Soviet Master of Sports title – in 1940.

Here's what the Lithuanian grandmaster Vladas Mikenas wrote about the Kemeri tournament and Petrovs (after his posthumous rehabilitation): "V. M. Petrovs was, of course, a brilliant chess player. He proved that at the Kemeri 1937 tournament, becoming a member of the elite chess circles. His deep chess understanding especially showed when he had white in the Catalan Opening. It was incredibly difficult to play against Petrovs' Catalan. I have no doubt: if not for the horrific years of the war, Petrovs would have achieved great successes in his favorite art of chess." However, Petrovs wasn't killed on a battlefield – he perished in one of Stalin's camps.

In memory of chess theoretician Aron Nimzowitsch, the son of a rich Riga merchant who emigrated to Germany, his relatives who stayed in Riga established a special prize – a silver cup – for the best game by a Latvian

Prizes from the Kemeri tournament: a silver cup from the Nimzowitsch family, as well as carved chess pieces and an amber-encrusted chess board from the President of Latvia Karlis Ulmanis

player against foreign opponents. Vladimirs Petrovs won this prize for his game against Rellstab.

The amber chess set, the Latvian president's prize for the tournament winner, and two cups, including the Nimzowitsch family one, are the only items I managed to preserve. This is all that remained from Vladimirs Mikhailovich Petrovs' chess career. *[And they remain in the possession of the Petrovs family as of the publication of the English version of this book.]*

The Kemeri 1937 tournament was the first time I met and got to know chess players. I look at the photos of all the tournament participants. I remember all their names, but I wasn't introduced to all of them.

Finally, Traveling Around Europe Together!

That year, Vladimirs Petrovs' chess career rose to a new level. His grandmaster title opened doors to elite tournaments, and he was in great form. In July 1937, we registered our marriage in the Riga registry office and went to the Stockholm Olympiad together. The wedding ceremony took place later, at Christmas in 1937, in Rezekne, my hometown.

The Stockholm Olympiad, according to Volodya, wasn't an especially valuable event from the chess point of view: the huge number of participants forced the organizers to establish a time control of 50 moves per 2.5 hours; such a playing tempo made creativity all but impossible, and most players couldn't show their strongest and richest play. Therefore, the competition in the Swedish Grand Hotel Royal was incredibly difficult. The participants had to play two games per day, which took 10 to 11 hours. The Latvian national team was weakened by the absence of Feigins, Bergs and Hasenfuss. Their replacements weren't as strong as them, so Petrovs and Apsenieks basically had to carry the whole team. Considering that Volodya constantly smoked at the board, what later happened when he returned to Riga was not surprising.

First, though, before the important game against Max Euwe at the Olympiad, Volodya decided to quit smoking. We lived in a hotel on Kungsgatan Street. In the night, he felt sick. He was covered by sweat, gasping for air, we could barely feel a pulse, and he had severe chills. We had to call for a doctor. I remember that the doctor spoke German well, so communication wasn't difficult. We told him how long Petrovs had been smoking and how many cigarettes he smoked each day. The doctor said that quitting cold turkey was not advised, and that this was the cause of his condition. He shouldn't try that again – at least during the tournament. Volodya was very happy when he heard that, saying that I shouldn't pester him about it anymore. He grabbed a cigarette and took a drag, and then chain-smoked several more. This left him

dizzy and even nauseous. In the morning, Volodya was weak and pale, and he
lost to Euwe. He never tried to quit smoking again after that, and, as long as
I remember him, he would always smoke when he sat at the chess board at
home.

In Stockholm, Petrovs learned that the tournament of eight of the world's
strongest chess players, scheduled for 25th August in Semmering, had been
moved to 8th September, and mostly to Baden bei Wien. The tournament
included Capablanca, Fine, Reshevsky, Flohr, Eliskases, Keres and Ragozin.

But our trip to Baden was in jeopardy. The consequences of the difficult
Stockholm Olympiad quickly showed themselves. Immediately after
returning to Riga, Vladimirs Mikhailovich was hospitalized – as he wrote to
me, an old tuberculosis process in his upper left lung became acute. Of course,
his constant smoking had something to do with that.

From Vladimirs Mikhailovich's letter to me, 21st August 1937:

*"Galya! Just don't worry. Your husband is very sick. What you were told in
the city clinic is not true. The captain, our military doctor, became so serious
when he saw the results of my X-ray that I got scared. He immediately sent
me to a military hospital and said that I was so seriously ill that I would
probably be discharged from military service. A tuberculosis process has again
become active in my upper lung, and it's very dangerous, more dangerous than
inflamed lymph nodes... It's now 7 p.m., and I'm going to the hospital at 10
p.m. I'm so afraid and sad... And Talia, my beloved sister, made me even sadder
– she says that I'll miss the Baden tournament as well. I'll have to spend a full
month in hospital.*

*Where now are our dreams about traveling to Baden together? I want to go
to Baden, I want it, I want it, and, of course, together with you!"*

Then, in letter from the military hospital dated just two days later, 23rd
August 1937, Volodya wrote to me that he would indeed be discharged from
the army for medical reasons. The letter that I received in Rezekne was nervy,
almost hysterical. The next day, he would undergo a medical commission that
discharged him from military service.

Quotes from the letter:

*"I'm a cripple! I have no right to tie you to a sick man. Junior and senior
doctors examined me yesterday and today. They took a blood count – there's
a fall to 4. They said that it wasn't that bad. I had an old process in my lung, it
almost closed, but the Olympiad activated it, and it started again in my upper
left lung. Does such a cripple have any right to the wonderful, gentle Galochka
whom I love very, very much?!*

*The junior doctor says that it's not that serious, that this process can be cured.
What I need now is rest, good food, fresh air, less sun, and no bathing. All the*

doctors say unanimously that I should quit smoking, but I (your Volodya is so bad) still smoke (very little, 5 papirosa cigarettes yesterday and only three today, even though it's 2 p.m. already). I'll have to quit. All in all, I feel well enough. I had no night sweats, but my palms were damp, and there's some general weakness – I get tired and want to lie down after just half an hour of walking in the park. For God's sake, don't tell anything to mother or Kolya. I'm a tuberculosis patient now, so, goodbye dreams about Rezhitsa[4]. What if I'm infectious and infect you all? The junior doctor, Gerhard, reassured me; he said that if I rest well in the next two weeks, I may even make it to Baden. Just think, what good am I for anything now? The senior doctor said that I should avoid everything until I fully recover...

What should I do about Baden? How to prepare for it? Where am I supposed to "rest"? No! No! I won't go to Rezhitsa to meet you! Yes, it's ridiculous! How quickly my military service ended! I'm so ashamed to tell anyone that I was discharged because of illness. I'm horribly ashamed before everyone and your family, but not before you! You're my only sun. Forgive me, Galochka, I haven't written anything about you, but I can't live without you..."

Perhaps his illness was the main reason for his setback in Baden. Of course, he exaggerated it greatly.

All European casinos, at least at the time, had to spend a certain percentage of their profits on cultural pursuits. Chess tournaments fitted the bill perfectly – relatively cheap, but highly popular events that attracted attention from the whole world. This was the main foundation for many chess tournaments of the era. When the biggest European casino in Baden decided to organize a chess tournament at short notice, nobody knew what tournament that would be, who would take part and what format would be used. The only thing that was guaranteed was Capablanca's participation. The early stage of the preparation was completely chaotic; many chess players received "false" invitations for a tournament that started on 25th August. Eventually, it was decided to dub the event "The Tournament of Eight Strongest Players in Semmering-Baden", hold a double round-robin and appoint Max Euwe as the arbiter. Later, though, Euwe had to depart urgently, and he was replaced by Spielmann. The tournament was held on 8th – 27th September 1937. The first four rounds were played in Semmering, and then the tournament was moved to the Baden casino. The tournament participants lived in the Gruner Baum Hotel.

For Vladimirs Petrovs, the Semmering-Baden tournament began with a crushing blow. First of all, I couldn't join him on the trip, and, secondly, he

---

4   The pre-1917 Russian name of Rezekne. – Translator

had to prove to everyone that his Kemeri success wasn't a fluke. In addition to all that, he "managed" to catch a cold.

Quotes from his letter from Baden, 13ᵗʰ September 1937:

"One draw in four games! I'm so ashamed and sad that I've stopped writing for the newspapers, and I'll never again write anything for anybody. Goodbye to all my dreams! Indeed, I was right when I said that your absence at the tournament would affect my play. I'm more than sure that were you present in Semmering, I would have accepted the draw against Reshevsky and wouldn't have taken risks against Flohr, with whom I could also have drawn and against whom I risked to play for a win only because I had already lost to Reshevsky. In addition, I'm very nervous and threw away an easy win against Keres, whom I'd outplayed in the opening and could literally have crushed in the middlegame. But I got into time trouble in the middle of the game and started making worse and worse moves.

Had you been in Semmering, I wouldn't have caught a cold. When I played Keres, I had a 37.7 Celsius fever. I still don't feel too well. I'm broken, mentally and physically. If only you could come...

I lost my nerve. Euwe tried to console me [the organizers managed to persuade a reigning world champion to work as an arbiter – a unique case in world chess history!], *saying that these losses were for my benefit, too, but the world is heartless and only looks at the results, and I'm not getting any results!*

Come as soon as you receive this letter! Never mind the money – we'll earn some! You see, your absence has already cost me money – at the very least, the money awarded to non-prizewinners for every point scored (30 lats per point, and I have already lost two – the same sum you would have spent on traveling). I'll pay for the return trip and the hotel – we'll earn enough money here. For

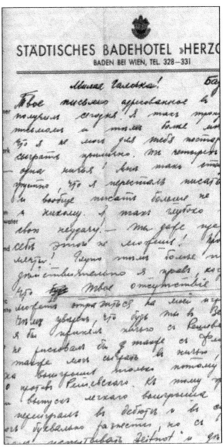

A letter from Petrovs to me from the Semmering-Baden tournament

God's sake, do not tell your mother that I have caught a cold. I'm still sneezing constantly, because I wasn't careful and never wore my coat, even though it was damp and misty here. It's always cloudy in Semmering in the autumn, because it's located in the highlands, but it's good in winter. Here in Baden, though, it's warm again. Roulette also cost me some money. At first I held on and avoided gambling, but after my losses, I wanted to distract myself a bit. I lost 70 schillings (i.e. 70 lats) in four days. I won't gamble anymore.

Please come, my love! I'm waiting, and as I wait for you, I promise to play well against Fine tomorrow, I have black, and I'll make a quiet draw. Let them try to defeat me. Come, my dear, by all means. Borrow some money in Riga if needed, I'll earn money in Riga and repay them. Tell your mother and father that Galya will be with Volodya, and everything will be fine. I'll book a room for you. Okay?!

Reshevsky and Mr. Euwe send their regards.

Yours for all life, Volodya."

Of course I went there. And Petrovs, after suffering a heavy mental blow in the first leg of the tournament – just 1.5 points out of a possible 7 – pulled himself together and got a 50% score in the second leg, i.e. 3.5 points. Considering the situation, everyone was surprised by Petrovs' ability to collect himself and overcome the setbacks. Even though this was Vladimirs Mikhailovich's intrinsic ability, I think that my arrival did influence matters this time. If only that tournament had included third and fourth legs as well... Nevertheless, Semmering-Baden was the first and last tournament in Petrovs' career where he finished last.

Capablanca's appearance impressed me mightily. He was incredibly handsome, elegant, slender, with blue eyes and dark hair. His smile was charming, even though he rarely smiled and was mostly unfriendly. Petrovs even got jealous of him. But Capablanca was very narcissistic. I didn't like his overconfidence, his feeling of superiority. I thought that he looked down on everyone and everything. I

Capablanca and his chess were the entire purpose of Olga's life

got utterly flustered in his presence. Capablanca once said to me that I looked like a little girl...

I'm holding a photo taken in Baden, depicting me, Raisa Flohr and Olga Capablanca (the widow of a Russian emigre, previously – Olga Chegodaeva). We are so different. Olga has very expressive eyes. A beautiful, majestic woman. Her beauty was of a woman loving, loved and very happy. She looked like a queen to me. Olga said that she was a duchess. Olga loved Capablanca madly, looked at him adoringly. She told me about her love for him many times. Capablanca, according to her, also loved her very much. I asked her what language they conversed in. She answered, "You don't need language for love, Galyusha." The pretty brunette, slender and petite Raisa, was completely overshadowed by her. Olga was very interested in the life of Russians in Latvia. She knew Russian literature well and I often asked her about Russian emigre writers. In my first year as a student, I had lived in Riga with my uncle, a well-known writer Sergey Rudolfovich Mintslov, who had been persuaded by Punga to move there from Yugoslavia, and I got to know many writers there, both living in Latvia and coming from abroad – so I had many topics to discuss with Olga. Our conversations with Raisa weren't as spiritual, so to say.

Raul and his chess were everything in Olga's life. Standing beside Olga and Raisa, I thought of myself as quite insignificant and unattractive. I swore to myself to be more like Olga, to take more interest in my husband's pursuits and his chess. Alas... Volodya consoled me, saying that I was his most beautiful queen.

I hated the adjourned games, especially if Volodya's position was worse. He sat up all night at the board in our room, getting almost no sleep, and then went to the play-off very tired. I couldn't distract him with anything, so I got angry and grumpy. Now, as I remember it, I realize that I was not sufficiently sensitive or attentive. My husband's chess life wasn't the meaning of our life for me. When I anxiously watched the demonstration boards at the tournaments and tried to predict the final result, I always counted how many pieces were left on the board. Even though Petrovs explained to me numerous times that the number of pieces does not always correspond to winning chances, I still couldn't kick the old habit. As soon as I looked at the board, I started counting them.

I remember playing roulette together with Keres in the Baden casino; I dropped a chip, and it rolled under the table. Forgetting about all propriety, I got down on my knees to search for it. The croupier looked at me reproachfully and said, "Madame..." I was very embarrassed. We immediately left afterwards. Paul berated me, said that I discredited him. Later, he told me and Petrovs that he had developed a fool-proof way to win at roulette.

With Petrovs and Najdorf in Warsaw, 1937

He indeed won often. When I asked him to explain his system, he said that it was too complex for a woman's mind. Later, he did reveal his secret, but his system still worked only for him.

I remember Paris in spring... Not far from the Louvre, there was the Cafe de la Regence, famous for chess activities. I ran to the Louvre at every opportunity, and Petrovs would spend all his free time in that cafe. I only went there once. Small, but cozy rooms. I heard that Robespierre and even Napoleon (before he became Emperor) used to play chess there. It turned out that bridge was played there as well. Petrovs was a strong bridge player and even represented Latvia at some tournaments. He loved the game at least as much as chess. He tried to teach me bridge as well... but, as in the case with chess, his efforts were futile.

In Paris, Petrovs introduced me to the French chess player Nicolas Rossolimo – he said that he was of Russian origin. I was surprised at his surname but I don't remember his explanation for it. He spoke Russian very well, albeit with an accent. He spoke it much better than I spoke French, so we talked in Russian. He was a young man, slender and handsome. We met again at another tournament, I think it was in Margate.

In Stockholm, Petrovs and I once went out to the countryside. We sat on big stones, with a view over the city. The day was wonderful. We dreamed about our future life together. I remember saying that I would like to travel somewhere just for the sake of traveling, without going to tournaments. "Where would you like to go?" Volodya asked. I was preparing for an exam on Egyptian history at the time, reading a lot of books. I was very interested in Egypt: dig sites, pyramids... He replied: "And I would like to travel all around Russia. The Caucasus, Crimea, Siberia! We don't know much about it, only from books." This wish did come true. Volodya didn't get to see the whole of Russia, but he did get to know the North...

I remember the positive and warm feelings from the time we spent with the Euwe family. They had two daughters, I remember one very well – a fair-haired, cute girl. I promised him and his wife to go and visit them sometime, but couldn't keep that promise...

In Vienna, we stayed in the chess player Spielmann's apartment. Everyone was very anxious – this was the time of Anschluss, the annexation of Austria by Germany. Spielmann lived alone and ate bread with jam for breakfast – he said that he couldn't afford anything more. The room was quite neglected, it was obvious that he was suffering material hardship. He was very sweet with us. He avoided talking about Hitler and Germany – it seems that even back then the Austrians feared speaking their mind. In the Vienna castle, Volodya was fascinated by the love story of Crown Prince Rudolf and Marie von Vetsera. On their suicide, he said that he would have done that too if someone had separated us. (I don't think he would have done that – he wasn't *that* romantic. He probably said that just for the sake of saying anything, he did like to exaggerate. Even back then, I often disbelieved his words deep in my heart.) We went to an amusement park and won a big teddy bear. When I disembarked in Riga holding that bear in my hands, it suddenly growled, and there was some trouble at customs because of that. We rode a Schneider steam locomotive. We also tried the Ferris wheel, and when we reached the very top, it stopped. They couldn't restart it for ages for some reason, and we got quite cold.

London, however, left a dismal impression. The perpetual fog was depressing. The city seemed too serious and tranquil, it was alien to our Russian souls. Paris and even Vienna, when we lived with Spielmann, felt much more familiar. I remember Volodya being warned by his London friends: you can say anything to anyone, but never mention the queen. We bought a suit for Volodya there, and a light-colored coat for me; it would turn gray and dusty towards the evening (I thought that this was caused by the perpetual fog). The adventures of this coat and me wearing it were truly "legendary": in Spain, it was pierced during a bullfight; in Prague, it was lost and suddenly found two days later; finally, it was burned during a student party in Lielvarde.

Who Needs Cotton?

Petrovs' trip to the Argentina Olympiad was the biggest and longest in the entire history of Latvian chess. The road to the Olympiad lay via the Netherlands, Belgium and the Atlantic Ocean. The host country, Argentina, chartered a special steamship for all European teams taking part in the competition. The ship was called *Piriapolis* and the trip took a whole month in one direction. The ship stopped in the Brazilian port Pernambuco, Rio de Janeiro, Santos, Uruguay's capital Montevideo and other cities.

"If *Piriapolis* hits a floating iceberg," Petrovs joked, "there will be literally no good chess players left in Europe..."

Piriapolis arrived at Buenos Aires in the early morning of 21st August, a little behind schedule. The Argentine capital met the chess players with its characteristic winter weather, 10–12°C. Our players settled in the Avenida Palace Hotel.

Petrovs achieved the best result on board one at this Olympiad (for the first time in his Olympiad career, he didn't lose a single game and therefore could compete for the individual medal. Only three players avoided losses: Alekhine, Capablanca and Petrovs). The gold medal, however, was awarded to the ex-world champion Capablanca. The reason was that Capablanca missed some matches of his national team: he only played 5 games in the semi-final, unlike Petrovs and Alekhine (6 games each), and he played 11 games in the final, winning 6. He avoided playing Alekhine, Keres and Eliskases.

Despite Capablanca playing only 16 games and scoring 11.5 points, the South American organizers awarded the medal to him. This was because they decided to count only the games played in the final, and there Capablanca's performance was indeed the strongest – 77.3%. Alekhine also played 16 games and scored 12.5 points, but he only played 10 games in the final, winning 5. Petrovs, like Capablanca, won 6 games in the final, but he played 13 games, which obviously lowered his percentage; overall, he played 19 games at the Olympiad, scoring 13.5 points. Unlike his main competitors, Petrovs couldn't afford to miss games – he had his team's best interests at heart.

As a result, thanks to all those "tricky calculations", Capablanca won the individual gold, Alekhine came second (even though he had the best overall point percentage, 78.1%), and Petrovs third. By the way, this was the only Olympiad Capablanca played in – seemingly only because he wanted to prove

The Latvian Olympic team, Buenos Aires, September 1939

his moral right to a world championship rematch with Alekhine. Petrovs missed only one game at the Olympiad – in the 8th round of the final. He didn't play at Alekhine's request: the world champion asked our grandmaster not to play against him, promising that France's second-strongest player, Gromer, would miss the match too. Thus, Latvia defeated France 2.5–1.5, and Alekhine got to keep his percentage intact. Latvia won its semi-final group and took seventh place out of 15 in the final.

When news about the war reached Buenos Aires, the most bizarre rumors started circulating there, fomented by the local press. On 2nd September, just a day after warfare started, it became known that "Warsaw was taken by storm". There was much turmoil among the players. It's sufficient to say that only about 40 percent of all European players returned home as soon as it ended for the readers to imagine how anxious everyone at the Olympiad was. Keres, like Petrovs, was offered some lucrative engagements, so he decided to postpone his return. The Latvian maestro Feigins feared transit through certain countries and lost his composure, but decided to bide his time. The Swedish players left on their steamship, and the Norwegians left on theirs. All German players, fearing that they would be forced to disembark in England, decided to stay in Buenos Aires. Two Polish players, Tartakower and Regedzinski, returned to Europe on the same steamship as the Latvian team, *Copacabana*, flying the Belgian flag. Tartakower went to Paris, and Regedzinski to Lodz, where he had a wife and three children.

So Volodya, the team captain, didn't bring back all the team members. Maestro Feigins was able to stay in Argentina because the Latvian team hadn't been issued a joint passport, so everyone had traveled on their own passports.

Twelve players who stayed played a tournament in Buenos Aires; others canceled their engagements and played a tournament in Rosario. Petrovs won, drawing against Eliskases and winning his other six games.

Copacabana was a commercial and passenger steamship. In addition to chess players, it carried oranges, coffee and 5,000 tons of cotton. In addition, *Copacabana* picked up the crew of a German steamship that was sunk near Montevideo by the English naval cruiser HMS *Ajax*. The *Copacabana* captain agreed to take the crew because it was comprised of Hungarians, Dutchmen and Belgians. Along the way, the captain recommended the sole German citizen to disembark somewhere. Soon, the *Copacabana* was detained by English forces near European shores and sent to Weymouth for inspection. When the Englishmen determined whom the cotton belonged to – it was addressed to some Swiss firm – the passengers were "let go". The chess players sat in Weymouth for four days on their ship, then they were politely asked to board a motorboat and transferred to another steamship, the *Persian*, which took them to Antwerp in four days (even though this distance was usually covered in 8–9 hours).

The journey across the North Sea was uneventful, if we discount the efforts of pilots who guided the ships through the minefields, and the passengers' emotions at seeing the sunken steamships belonging to various countries. The *Persian* moved carefully, over shallower waters. The passengers sometimes saw the noses of torpedo boats sticking out of the water.

Games of bridge helped to kill time. But the life jackets they had to keep close at all times constantly reminded them of the circumstances in which they were traveling.

Several times, the captain sounded false alarms, and the passengers put on their life jackets and boarded the lifeboats... Volodya's adventures hadn't stopped on the road – they continued in Riga, too. We – some of Volodya's friends, a couple of chess players and I – would head to the train station to meet the trains twice per day, but we miscalculated somehow and missed the night train. And this was precisely the train on which the Latvian team came home. As they disembarked, they only saw a single Riga chess player, who was known for his nocturnal lifestyle... And as he took a walk after his "dinner" at two o'clock in the morning, he decided to visit the train station. Due to his absentmindedness, he, of course, forgot to tell Volodya that I had moved home in the interim... On a dark night, Volodya went to Pardaugava, called and knocked on his own door, but nobody opened. Volodya got to the nearest phone and woke up one of his friends with the question, "Do you know, by any chance, where I now live?"

To make life easier for me and my daughter – Volodya only got back home 15 weeks later – Sergejs Karcevs had offered me an apartment in his building on Matisa Street. The night security guard greeted Petrovs with much suspicion.

"Have you come from America? Well, they all say that..."

When the security guard saw the suitcases, he did open the doors. He kept his eyes on Petrovs until I hugged and kissed him. Only after that did the security guard, obviously embarrassed, return to his room.

Instead of a gold medal, Petrovs brought back... a cosmetics diploma awarded in Paris to some lady. Here's how it happened: during a change of night train in dark Cologne, the luggage disappeared. It was impossible to find it in the darkness. When the porter finally found the suitcases and brought them to the train, he added an extra brown suitcase from the luggage of some woman heading to Riga to Petrovs' belongings. Petrovs decided to take the suitcase with him and found a diploma and other goods there. The suitcase belonged to a hairdresser from the Max salon on Brivibas Street. She had completed some courses in Paris. Later, I personally handed her that suitcase.

Our short life together was fun, fascinating and happy. I accompanied my husband to chess tournaments. We traveled a lot, saw a lot, met the most interesting people. Meeting Alekhine, Euwe, Flohr, Capablanca, Keres was unforgettable. We became friends with many of them. Now, when I turn the pages of my life and remember my family, which was obliterated so ruthlessly, the old wounds open again and start bleeding.

Volodya was a good family man. He so wanted me to be beside him as he analyzed games! "Can't you learn to knit or embroider, or something? It would be so good to have you sitting beside me!" And I proved time and again that I just couldn't do that. I did try, but when Volodya saw my attempt to knit a sweater for our daughter, he said that I should make a cover for a coffee pot from that thing.

Volodya liked to eat, he was a gourmand. He had a voracious appetite, rubbing his hands together before downing a tiny shot of cold vodka, and would joke heartily after drinking. As his friends used to say, "you get an appetite just by looking at him". We often took lunch and dinner in restaurants.

The prices weren't high, and we could afford that. Every restaurant and even small cafe in Riga had its own famous signature dish. And since there were a lot of them in the city, we had a very wide choice.

Yes, this was a happy life – happy until 1941, when the sinister arms of Stalin's executioners reached our family.

A Century-Long Show

The husband of Petrovs' sister was the first victim. He was arrested in Riga, and his trace disappeared in the NKVD basements on Stabu Street; later, when the German army left, his photo in prison robes was found in the courtyard. Then my dear uncle, Hermans Andreevich Punga (the husband of my mom's sister), was arrested, too.

I feel obliged to dedicate some paragraphs to his blessed memory. He was a most interesting man with a remarkable biography. An ethnic Latvian, born in Liepaja, he was once a prominent member of the Social Democratic Party, spent quite a bit of time abroad, was arrested several times and sent to internal exile, but escaped. By chance, he was introduced to Chertkov, Tolstoy's secretary – they were friends for 15 years. My uncle traveled with him to England, serving as a tutor to Chertkov's son, Dmitry. In England, thanks to his friend's support, he obtained a higher education and became an eminent engineer. He knew Tolstoy himself as well, visiting him in Yasnaya Polyana numerous times. Punga once published his recollections of that period of his life. When my uncle was arrested and thrown into Warsaw prison, Tolstoy's family interceded in his favor. I remember a figurine of Tolstoy leaning on his walking staff on my uncle's desk, with a dedication, "To dear Hermans Andreevich Punga from Leo Tolstoy."

It was in Chertkov's English house that my uncle met my mother's sister, Elena Khristoforovna. They got married and relocated to the

Hermans Andreevich Punga – the Finance Minister in Cakste's government

Urals, where Punga became director of the famous Pashkov glass factories. My childhood memories begin with the Urals – they're connected with the Punga family: my mom brought me and my sister to visit them. Those were uncertain times. The revolution happened as we were there. My father Mikhail Mikhailovich Zenets, a railway engineer, was the son of a well-known medical professor from St. Petersburg. He was a port manager in Feodosia, living separately from our family, and I don't remember him much. Then my father died, and our fate became inextricably tied with the family of my uncle, who brought us to Latvia in 1921. Punga became the Finance Minister in Cakste's government, and then served as a diplomat in the USSR, Germany and England. He retired in 1939 and went back to Latvia. He was arrested in early 1941 and died in the Riga Central Prison on 22nd April 1941. *[Galina Mikhailovna only managed to obtain his death certificate in the mid-1990s – Vladimir Dedkov.]* I learned from one of the men who shared a cell with him that my uncle was brought back half-dead after interrogation. We can only imagine which methods of interrogation were used, especially considering that my uncle was a well-known man. After one interrogation, Punga was not brought back... They didn't get to sentence him – apparently, they tortured him to death before he could be taken to court.

On 18th October 1996, a cross was erected beside Riga Central Prison, on a symbolic grave of everyone who was tortured to death, killed or died on their own in the cells and basements. People always bring flowers to that grave. May your memory last forever too, my dear uncle Hermans!

His arrest shook us all to the core, and we were in constant fear for our other family members. Who's going to be next? This thought gnawed on our minds, made us lose sleep, and didn't let us live calmly or breathe freely.

In 1940, after Latvia's annexation, the country's chess life also took a sharp turn. After the first year of Soviet rule, the future was not clear yet, but Petrovs, as a chess player who could calculate several moves ahead, immediately realized that he wouldn't be able to represent Latvia in international tournaments anymore. Still, a new, unknown world of Soviet chess opened before him. It would have been so much better had he never known that world...

Volodya finished in tenth place the 12th Soviet Championship. "If the genius Keres only managed to share 12th–13th place when he debuted in Moscow in 1939, and showed some progress this time to take 4th place, the one who took 10th place on the first try has nothing more to wish for," he said. Of course, much more was expected from him – he possessed solid knowledge and great positional understanding. As Levenfish wrote at the time in *64*, Vladimirs lost his composure after defeats to Boleslavsky and Smyslov when he had won positions in both games. Otherwise, he would have taken a higher place.

Publicly, Petrovs himself cited "a lack of practice and constant time trouble" as the reason for his poor performance but I think that this wasn't the whole truth. Of course, after the Flohrs told him about Moscow, that you should fear your every word there, that they listen to everything, know everything, that you should be wary of any new acquaintance, Volodya, who was quite a worrier anyway, became mistrustful and morose in respect of all things Soviet.

When we returned from Hamburg, I told Petrovs how Terletsky, the Soviet consul, had invited Uncle Hermans onto a Soviet steamship, and how enraptured I was with everything (I showed him the book *How the Steel Was Tempered*, given to me by Terletsky; later, we both read the book). Volodya thought for some time, then said, "I think that this was all *for show*. We know nothing about the country. Only rumors, rumors and rumors... Wouldn't I like to see everything for myself, get to know and understand it." The dream came true... He did get to see everything for himself and did get to know everything.

Before going to the 12th Soviet Championship, Petrovs decided to take an active role in the reorganization of the Latvian Chess Union, but upon his return, he was not permitted to join the organizational efforts.

Vladimirs Mikhailovich brought some proposals from Leningrad. The first was to play a correspondence match between Leningrad and Riga or hold a tournament of the city trade unions. The second, immediately after the Baltic Team Championship, was to organize a 20-board match between Leningrad and the joint team of the Baltic republics. Nothing of the sort happened, however. Petrovs was pushed aside... He quickly realized what was expected from him in political and social life in Soviet Latvia. He was just confronted with the fact that the direction of chess development was already approved by the new leadership.

But he was only barred from organizational work. Petrovs still continued to play in all tournaments of the Latvian republic, but... in parallel with work. The first Latvian SSR Championship was held in the building of the Riga Exchange. As Petrovs told the press, he and the Riga master L. Dreibergs made a huge sacrifice by taking part in such a serious competition without taking leave from their main job. Dreibergs was a chemical engineer and got to the tournament straight from the factory. And Petrovs came to the tournament straight from the registry office, where he worked as a deputy manager. Of course, nobody could expect great sporting achievements in such circumstances. Moreover, Volodya himself treated this event as mere training, and when he finally pulled himself together, it was too late. We should also remember that Petrovs had to carry out some serious theoretical work as well: he analyzed the games of the 12th Soviet Championship for Levenfish's book. This obviously affected his play in a negative way, and he only took 4th place.

In 1941, Vladimirs Petrovs became the chess column editor in the most popular Latvian magazine, *Atputa*. There was an interesting line of succession there: the first editor, right until his death, was Hermanis Matisons (the first Latvian master); after him, Fricis Apsenieks (the second Latvian master) worked as the editor until he succumbed to an incurable disease; and, finally, Vladimirs Petrovs (the third Latvian master) took up the reins for a short time.

In May 1941, soon after Punga's arrest, Petrovs was invited to the Soviet Championship semi-final in Rostov-on-Don. Either he had some premonition or was just anxious because of the latest events, but he didn't want to go. One of Volodya's female colleagues in the registry office told me that as well. I couldn't go with him because I had to take state exams, and so fate had it that he went alone. My husband said his goodbyes for ages, instructing me to watch my health, not to get too tired, and to take care of our daughter. I look in the window, watching him get in the car; then he suddenly returns and asks me to give him a tennis racket – to challenge Keres, he said. He kisses us, makes the sign of the cross with a big golden crucifix which he always wore on his chest, takes my photo with the infant Marina with him, says goodbye and leaves. Leaves forever... His last words to me were, "Just wait, I'll be back, and you'll already have your master's degree. Don't try to celebrate without me! We'll do it together. Wait for a big gift..." He never came back home. War tore us apart...

Curse this year, 1941! My family was devastated that year, the start of suffering and sorrows.

The Rostov-on-Don semi-final was about halfway through. Decisive battles were ahead. The morning of

My photo with baby Marina, which Volodya took with him and which I got back 56 years later

Sunday, 22ⁿᵈ June, came. Some players were finishing their adjourned games, others were preparing for the next round, but then, at 12:00, the radio announced, "War!"

Unlike the checkers players, who also held the semi-finals of their national championship there in Rostov, the chess players couldn't finish the tournament. The players who served in the Red Army got immediately recalled to their military units. The reservists hurried to their units as well. To be honest, nobody was in any frame of mind to play, especially the players from the Baltic region and Western Ukraine – they couldn't return home anymore. After round 8, the tournament was officially called off. Volodya, together with Koblenz and the organizer Janis Fride, only managed to reach Velikie Luki. They were removed from the train there – the path to Latvia was closed.

Dr. Nikolajs Vasilyevich Lobovikovs with a tamed jackdaw, Ricky, who flew away on the day of my wedding. "Two jackdaws left home today," he said [the diminutive form of the author's name, Galka, means jackdaw in Russian]

In fact, my beloved parents became the next victims, in the infamous June Deportation. My mother had married Dr. Nikolajs Vasilyevich Lobovikovs in 1929, and we moved to the town of Rezekne, where he lived and worked. The doctor loved me and my sister as much as a real father. We sincerely loved him, and I owe him for my amazing, happy youth, for the education he gave me, for the warm and cozy fatherly home... They were taken from Rezekne on 14ᵗʰ June 1941. On this day, my old life was irrevocably destroyed...

Before the exams, I had taken my daughter Marina to my parents' home. I had four free days before the last exam, and I decided to pay her a visit for a day. On 13ᵗʰ June, I took the evening train from Riga and got to Rezekne in the early morning. On my way from the station, to my shock, I saw a line of trucks filled with people with some bundles, sacks, bales... There were men and women, old folks and children. Many were crying. I couldn't understand what was going on, I just stopped in my tracks when I saw my friends and acquaintances in the trucks. What happened? Where are they being taken to? Why?

I ran towards home, sensing imminent danger. Nikolajs Vasilyevich was carrying out a surgery in the hospital. My mom was very glad to see me, and she went to the kitchen to make me some breakfast. My daughter was sleeping sweetly. I said nothing to my mother about what I had seen in the city, not wanting to scare her. And then the doorbell rang. I opened the door... Soviet military men in blue peaked caps stood on the doorstep. There was a truck before the house, with some armed soldiers. My vision got misted up.

They asked for the doctor, then sent someone to the hospital for him. Then they told me to call my mother and started to search the house. My mom hadn't heard the doorbell, and I had no time to call her – she came into the room smiling, not suspecting anything, with breakfast for me – as far as I remember, it was scrambled eggs. I couldn't forget her huge, horrified gray eyes when she saw me surrounded by the blue peaked caps. The doctor was brought home, then we were told that we had 40 minutes to gather our belongings. They warned us to take warm clothes, because we weren't going to some resort, and then read an order for Dr. Lobovikovs, my mother A. K. Lobovikova and Marina Petrova to be deported from the Latvian SSR. What happened next? Later, I tried for ages to recall what exactly happened after that. I tried to convince them that there was an error in the order, that Marina was my 2 year-old daughter, and my name was Galina Petrova (by the way, I couldn't actually prove that because I had no documents on me). I asked them to either leave my daughter with me or take me with them, but they replied that they had no orders to do that, and if I wanted to go with them, I had to submit an application at my

My sister Tusya with our family favorite, the beauty Lo

place of registration, i.e. in Riga. They were led away... I remained alone in a trashed house, it was raining outside, and our dog was running from room to room and howling... I found some cigarettes in the doctor's table and smoked, for the first time in my life. Where to run, where to search for them? Whom to ask to remain in the house in case they brought my daughter back? My head was spinning, all my energy had left me, and I felt nauseous.

And suddenly the phone rang. A woman spoke in a muted voice; when she learned that I was the doctor's daughter, she told me that there was a train at Rezekne-2 station, and people were being brought to it, the Lobovikovs included. Stumbling, crying, I ran to the station like mad. Our dog Lo followed me. There was indeed a very long train of gloomy, heated railcars with grates on tiny windows. It looked endless. Armed guards walked along the train, we weren't allowed to approach the railcars. Trucks arrived one after another, the guards got their passengers to disembark and shoved them onto the train. God, how many familiar faces! It seemed that the entire city population had been brought here. I ran back and forth along the train, trying to find my parents. The guards pushed me away; they also drove away the bloody-eyed dog that ran around, growling, barking and occasionally jumping at the guards. I thought that they would shoot him.

The doctor was put into one of the first railcars – Antons Antonovich Tallats-Kelis, a friend of our family and the head of Latvia's Poland Department, shouted that to me through a window. They sat together. His wife, Olga Alexeevna, the headmistress of a Polish school in Rezekne, was also somewhere in the train with her daughter. The men were separated, and they knew nothing about their wives and children. Later, Tallats-Kelis died in Vyatlag in Dr. Lobovikovs' arms.

My mother and Marina were in one of the last railcars. I can't remember whom I addressed, where I ran, whom I begged to give my daughter back, but someone took pity on us and returned her to me. It was probably God's providence that led me to Rezekne on that fateful day and helped save my daughter. I ran away with the child, without saying goodbye to my parents, without saying anything to anybody, without waiting for the train to depart. The eyewitnesses later said that the dog ran after the departing train.

I never returned to their home. It remained there with open doors, and then it was nationalized. I took the first train to Riga. Then the war started. The German army invaded Latvia. Several weeks passed, and suddenly another friend of our family, the owner of the Moskovskaya drugstore, called me from Rezekne. She said that when she came to the drugstore in the morning, she saw the dying Lo on the doorstep. How long did the dog pursue the train, what obstacles did he cross, when did he finally lose scent of his owners?

Even the dog couldn't tolerate the horror of that happening. That's how our beautiful Lo died – pining for his loving and caring owners.

The Wartime Tournaments

Meanwhile, Petrovs also stayed in the USSR. He played in tournaments, won prizes and knew nothing about what was happening to his family. The first big wartime tournament was of course the 1941 Moscow Championship, held in November and December. Without a doubt, this tournament was more of a political act than a sporting event. Mazel won the championship, and Vladimirs finished as runner-up. According to V. G. Povarov, a match between Alatortsev and Petrovs had also been scheduled for September in Moscow, but all he could find in the press of the time was that the first game was adjourned.

The second major wartime tournament was held on 17th February – 12th March 1942 in Moscow. It was a double round-robin featuring eight masters. Bondarevsky won, and Petrovs finished second.

Sverdlovsk hosted a tournament on 22nd March – 10th April 1942, with six masters and five first-category players taking part. First place was mostly contested between Boleslavsky, who was considered the heavy favorite, and Ragozin, who was in great form, even though he only came from the besieged Leningrad two weeks earlier. Ragozin ultimately won, and Petrovs again came second. This tournament was the last complete one in Vladimirs Mikhailovich Petrovs' career; at the very least, there were no further mentions of his chess activity, either by eyewitnesses or in the press. Four months later, in August, he was arrested. According to some unverified sources, he was taken away straight from the chess board at some tournament. I haven't managed to find out what kind of tournament or competition this was.

Here is Petrovs' resume that he submitted when he applied for a job with the letters department of the USSR Council of People's Commissars' Radio Committee *[Voronkov in his book explains this document's origin]*:

"I was born in Riga on 27th September 1908, in a worker's family. My father worked at a shoe factory. I graduated from secondary school in 1925 and enrolled in the law school of Latvian University, which I graduated from in spring 1940. I took breaks in my education for financial reasons.

Since 1924, I have taken various jobs, mostly giving private lessons. I worked as a journalist since 1929, mostly reporting on sports and chess. In 1933–1941, I worked in Riga's civilian organs in various capacity; in the last few years, I have worked as an administrator of registry offices in the Latvian SSR. In 1926, I earned the chess master's title, which determined the next steps in my life: I took part in international tournaments and Olympiads in various countries of Central and Western Europe and America.

Since 1940, I've been playing in Soviet tournaments. In the Latvian SSR, I worked for and with the *Proletarskaya Pravda* newspaper and *Atputa* magazine; in Moscow, for the *64* chess newspaper, *Shakhmaty v SSSR*, *Krasny Sport*, and *Moskovsky Bolshevik*, and for the English magazine *CHESS*.

In September 1941 I volunteered for the newly formed Latvian Riflemen Division near Gorky. I was dismissed for being of no use to the Red Army and was left to carry out public work with a deferral of conscription until 31.12.19.. (the last two digits were cut out by the hole puncher). From 1st January 1942 until 15th June 1942 I worked in the Moscow City Committee of Dynamo as an aide to the Commander. I am married. I have never been a member of any political organization.

Moscow, 18th June 1942. V. M. Petrovs."

Vladimirs Petrovs' dates of birth and death in foreign sources were mostly wrong. Based on information from official sources, we can now correct them: Vladimirs Mikhailovich Petrovs, an ethnic Russian, was born in Riga on 27th September 1908 and died in a Soviet labor camp (somewhere near Kotlas) on 26th August 1943.

One of Latvia's most prominent players was and still remains a *persona non grata* in chess history.

From autumn 1942, the Soviet Union turned Vladimirs Petrovs into a "non-person". For instance, an article about chess tournaments in 1942 never even mentions Petrovs' name among the participants of the Moscow and Sverdlovsk tournaments. Judging by the Sverdlovsk report, one would think that the second prize was never awarded.

In 1945, when I got back to Riga, I immediately ran to our flat on Matisa Street. As I entered the courtyard, I was greeted by sheets of paper with game scores and notes written by my husband, scattered by the wind. The new "owners" of the flat had acted like conquerors: the former owner, the "enemy of the people", was imprisoned, and all his confiscated belongings were "bought out" from the state. After some insistent knocking, an obviously drunken man in boxer shorts opened the door. When I asked for specific items to remember my husband by, this shining example of the "new culture" said, "They got lost during our last drinks party!"

I got further proof that the flat had been looted in the Ministry of Finances, when on the table of some department head, I saw a familiar-looking stationery holder set that was presented to Petrovs by fellow soldiers from his military unit for his Kemeri tournament win. The list of goods sold

That same stationery holder set that was gifted to Petrovs by fellow soldiers from the sixth Riga platoon which by some strange means found itself on the table of a department head at the Ministry of Finances

from the apartment that I obtained in the ministry obviously didn't feature the library, the paintings, the grand piano, the furniture set from the office, or the prizes won by my husband.

The Maestro's Last Game

Petrovs was arrested on 31st August 1942 and, according to a decision of a special council on 3rd February 1943, sentenced to 10 years of labor camps for anti-Soviet propaganda. He was arrested after a denunciation. I learned about that from Petrovs' case file, which I finally managed to obtain in Moscow in 1996. I decided not to publicize the names of the snitches, but I can say that there were three of them – three Moscow masters who played in several Soviet Championships. *Sapienti sat...*[5]

---

5 Unfortunately those pages from the case file that the author was allowed to photocopy and are kept in her archive do not contain the names of the snitches, while the case file in the KGB archives in Russia now contains an empty envelope where the denunciations are supposed to be kept, so we were unable to confirm the names. We can only speculate about the fate of the missing documents – Vladimir Dedkov

For the rest of my life, I used all possible channels (published notices, and wrote to camps and newspapers) to search for those who were imprisoned together with Petrovs or met him on the way to his Calvary. Only in March 1990, thanks to Voronkov, at the time the head of the *Shakhmaty v SSSR* magazine archive department, did I manage to find Alfred Martynovich Mirek, a doctor of art history, who shared the cell at Lubyanka with my husband. From him, I learned what happened to Petrovs. I was so anxious before this meeting; I wanted to know everything and I feared that it would open all the unhealed wounds once again.

The following text by Alfred Mirek was first published in Russian in *Shakhmaty v SSSR* No. 9, 1990 in an article entitled "Encounter at Lubyanka" *[and it was published in English in Voronkov's book mentioned earlier]*:

The turnover in the cell I wound up in was rather quick. This was an assembly point – a kind of hub where prisoners were sorted. The initial interrogations almost immediately determined the ultimate fate of the arrested.

In the morning, when I came to and cooled down somewhat, I started looking at the surrounding people. Almost everyone – there were around ten people in the cell – slept while sitting or reclining. Especially those who had returned from the night interrogation. Only one guy was wide awake – a chubby, stout man who sat at the open barred window with a view of the courtyard. He regularly got good deliveries (the only one in the cell) and behaved rather cheekily, with barely concealed superiority. A joker, "everybody's buddy". He would give some people treats, befriending them and getting them to talk, but would push others away with rudeness and mockery. A man, seemingly a worker, who sat beside me, nodded disdainfully towards him and said quietly, "He's a plant, don't say too much..." I looked at the guy involuntarily, and he asked me with an arrogant smile, "What have you come with, young man?" and threw me a *sushka*. The *sushka* fell on the floor. I turned away.

And then another victim of the sweep entered the cell – yes, the sweep, since he had arrived without any luggage, as though from a neighboring room. A young, square-built man, calm, collected and fit like a sportsman. He wore a dark suit, the collar of his shirt was unbuttoned. *[I remember – this is probably the same pinstriped suit we bought in London. It was his Sunday best suit, which he was supposed to wear at the championship. Where was he taken? Where did they find him? He didn't play at the Kazan tournament – perhaps they arrested him on the way there – G. M. Petrova-Matisa.]* He had no belongings with him, not even a coat or a hat. He sat down, looked around and introduced himself,

"Petrovs, a chess player". I had only heard of Botvinnik, Lasker and Capablanca back then, so the name didn't impress me at all. I wasn't a big fan of chess, even though I obviously did know what it was.

Our "joker" saw the newcomer, surveyed him with an experienced eye and decided that he was a worthy client. He immediately approached Petrovs, introduced himself as an engineer and, saying something enthusiastic about chess, dragged him to his bunk bed (in this cell, they resembled trestle beds with wooden planks). He took out a very worn-out chessboard, pieces – or, to be precise, a mock-up of pieces, made out of checkers – added some buttons to replace missing pieces, and offered to play a game. Petrovs readily agreed. He was surprisingly calm and looked like a sociable man. They put the board onto the windowsill and sat down on the trestle bed. The engineer constantly asked questions, and Petrovs gave terse answers. It was obvious that his mind was somewhere far away, and that he was playing almost automatically. After playing three or four games, which he won easily, the grandmaster (the nickname his opponent came up with) sat down to rest.

It was late in the evening. The feeder – a small window in the door that opened "sandwich-style" – opened, and two inmates were called out: Petrovs and another one. Petrovs came back two hours later, confused, tired and dejected. His short dark hair, which obviously hadn't been combed for a while, now pointed in different directions. He sat with his head slightly down, pushing his palms together. I clearly remember his deep, concentrated stare. A stupid person facing idiocy and injustice loses any power over themselves and easily panics; a clever person, on the other hand, mobilizes internally, tries to comprehend the reasons for what's going on, to understand what to do now...

I took off my overalls, rolled them, put them under my head and lay asleep on the floor. Nobody had called for me yet...

Moscow, 1942. The last photo of a free Petrovs (from the Sverdlovsk tournament bulletin, 24th April). It was brought to Riga by a Moscow chess player after the war and, unable to find me, he entrusted it to the chess master Solmanis. Petrovs reportedly told the chess player, "I feel I won't see my family anymore, so let me look at them at least from the photo..."

The next day, Petrovs was again called for interrogation, a bit earlier this time. He came back in the same state as the day before, his face was gray. It was also obvious that he was very hungry. The food rations in the jail were minimal, and he had also missed supper (a spoon of porridge and hot water). It was there, in the Lubyanka inner jail, that I first experienced the feeling of constant hunger that's only aggravated after every meal.

Petrovs sat next to an elderly worker, my bunk bed neighbor. He sat in deep thought for some time, and then started telling him about himself. My neighbor listened intently, only asking some tactful questions when Petrovs fell silent. The conversation was essentially between the two of them, and I only sat beside them and listened.

It turned out that he was a real grandmaster, a well-known Latvian chess player. In the 1920s and 1930s he played in many tournaments – in Paris, the Hague, Stockholm, other places. After Latvia joined the Soviet Union, and the war started, he worked as a translator in the army (he said he knew several languages). Then he played in tournaments in Sverdlovsk and the Volga Region. All in all, the investigator had a lot to work with – what he said was not only enough to incriminate him with the infamous Article 58.10 (anti-Soviet campaigning and propaganda), but also to accuse him of contacting foreigners, espionage in the army, etc. Even if you had no imagination at all, this was enough to get ten people imprisoned.

During the second interrogation, the investigator, according to Petrovs, was rather interested in his last visit to Latin America. If I recall correctly, it was about Argentina and Mexico. I'll try to quote this interrogation fragment as well as I remember it from Petrovs' words.

The interrogator (by the way, he was from a Baltic republic as well) asks, "Whom did you meet there? And do not try to hide anything, so to say."

"You know well whom I met there and my results, they were reported in the press. What would I hide about that and why?"

Petrovs maintained his dignity and some disregard for his interviewer, still thinking that this arrest was just a misunderstanding, a folly of some bureaucrat who had received an anonymous denunciation.

"Whom else did you meet?" the interrogator continued.

"Many people."

"That's the point. Name them."

"Everyone? By name?"

"Yes, and don't you dare to omit anyone, 'forget', so to say. What did you talk to them about, what did you ask them about? Which, so to say, instructions did they give you? And what did you, so to say, promise them?.."

This obtrusive, blunt "so to say", as I remember, annoyed Petrovs greatly. But he realized that he shouldn't have paid attention to that. The main point was to understand what the investigator wanted from him! And so he explained patiently that nobody had instructed him to do anything, he didn't have talks of that kind with anyone, asked nobody for anything and never planned to...

Even as he recounted all that, Petrovs couldn't hide his indignation and started to get wound up. In such a situation, the more honest and decent the person was, the harder it was for them to get through all that, to take part in such an absurd event.

From that conversation, we learned that he had been arrested about a week earlier, somewhere on the Volga. When he learned that he was being transported to Moscow, Petrovs calmed down. They'll surely get everything sorted out there. He was looking forward to meeting a Moscow investigator – that's why he was so calm in the cell during his jail chess debut. And the moment when the investigator introduced himself encouraged him – he was a compatriot, after all. But the joy was short-lived. Petrovs quickly realized that the investigator was a typical smug scumbag. And then it only got harder and harder.

In the following long pause, I asked him where he was from, where his home was. In Riga, he said. And he hadn't seen any of his belongings ever since his arrest. Even the photo of his wife and daughter had disappeared – the only thing that still reminded him of home...

Of course, the Lubyanka interrogations didn't consist solely of soulcrushing talks. I don't know exactly how they extracted confessions from Petrovs, but I can cite my own experience to give the readers a glimpse of the "investigation methods" of the time. The interrogations were held only at night. With persistence, which was quite puzzling to me, the investigator repeated the same thing all over again, "Will you talk, bandit?" (or sometimes "thief", for a change). I had a feeling that he didn't know himself exactly what he needed to hear from me or what I was meant to tell him... Once, probably trying to make things quicker, he took a pistol from his desk drawer and started running circles around me, waving the gun and screaming, "I'll shoot you!" Finally, he stopped behind me. I instinctively shrank, waiting for him to shoot me. And then he suddenly hit me on the head with the pistol grip. During another interrogation, the investigator decided to use an even "funnier" way of getting me to talk: he came up to me and suddenly pressed a burning cigarette into my neck...

The times were extremely tense in the country, and there, in isolation from the whole world, they seemed exaggeratedly dismal and sinister. In that jail, we were occasionally, but not often, escorted outside to take a walk. A

A photo of Petrovs from the criminal file

small courtyard was surrounded by tall walls from all four sides. There was a long balcony for the guards on the left of the exit, along the second floor.

On that sunny day, seven or eight of us, including Petrovs, were led outside, and as soon as we started to walk in a circle, someone commanded, "Turn to the wall, walk closer to it. Hands behind head!" Then soldiers entered the door beside us and walked to the opposing wall (we could hear the stomps on the ground and the clatter of guns). I looked at the wall without seeing it, fearing the worst: I knew from books and movies that sometimes, in critical situations, they "eliminated" prisoners. With my peripheral vision, I saw tense, unmoving faces to my left and right. "Should it really happen on such a sunny, quiet, warm fall day! On the other hand, 'fall' is quite symbolic", I thought, distracting myself from the petrified waiting. At this moment, we heard another command, "Hands behind backs, start walking!" Before we even recovered, we unconsciously, mechanically started walking by the courtyard walls. It turned out that it was time for a change in the security shift, and this ritual was used as a safety precaution in such cases.

This was my second and last walk in Lubyanka jail. It was also the last time I saw Grandmaster Petrovs. In the evening, he was called for interrogation and never returned to our cell. It seems that they had started to work on him in earnest. During these two weeks, he became rather haggard and gradually got the sense that he was doomed.

As I learned later, my husband was sent to the Butyrka prison and got completely broken there. Five months at Lubyanka and Butyrka were enough – on the way to Vorkuta, he, already mortally ill, was taken off the train at some transfer station and soon died.

That game at Lubyanka was apparently the last in the grandmaster's life. It's unlikely that he ever got an opportunity to sit at his beloved chess board again in the remainder of his short life. Petrovs' sentencing document that I received upon request says, "The charges against your husband were based on cases of his expressing his unhappiness with living conditions in the Baltic republics after they joined the USSR".

Not Subject to Rehabilitation

The Latvian SSR Prosecutor's office twice refused to posthumously rehabilitate him. First in response to my request in 1959, and then to that of our daughter, Marina Vladimirovna Petrova-Dedkova, in 1967. The text of the refusal was as follows: "According to the case files and the verification performed in 1959, Petrovs V. M. was justifiably arrested in 1942 and sentenced in 1943 for anti-Soviet propaganda, and he is not subject to rehabilitation. Latvian SSR Deputy Prosecutor Chibisov." After that, my daughter quit Komsomol as a gesture of protest, resentment and indignation, which led to trouble for her in her institute – she didn't get to graduate afterwards. Later, she couldn't find a job – everyone either refused outright or found some excuses.

In 1997, I managed to obtain Petrovs' archive case file, which was kept in Moscow. So after 56 years, I finally held that photo with my daughter again, the confiscation of which was taken so badly by my husband... I also received his last photos. I read and re-read the case file, and it occasionally seemed to me that I was going insane. The accusations were heavy and preposterous, and Petrovs emphatically denied everything. I was especially upset by my husband's answers about his marital status. He said that he was married to me from 1937 to February 1941 and then got a divorce. His father died in pre-war Latvia. His sister, Natalia, was evacuated to the USSR, and he knew nothing about her whereabouts. How could he have said such nonsense! Maybe my husband was going insane from interrogations? But after several sleepless nights, speculation and reflection, it became clear to me... "Ah, poor you! You haven't gone insane, haven't lost your mind, haven't made a mistake – you just distanced yourself from us, you saved us all!"

The life of Vladimirs Mikhailovich Petrovs was just a drop in the ocean of suffering, agony and sacrifices that engulfed the country.

He never got to know what happened to his family, which fell victim to the bloody regime, and what torments it had to live through. Fate was merciful to him at least in that.

Perhaps if Petrovs had died of natural causes or accident, I wouldn't have suffered from such pain, such a bleeding wound for years, but it's hard to get over the fact that he effectively died by the decision of some "committee" and then, like millions of other victims, was fully acquitted and rehabilitated.

In late 1988, the veteran Latvian chess player Igor Zhdanov mentioned Petrovs at a lecture for the first time, referring to him as a strong player who left a big mark on the development of Latvian chess. He analyzed some of his games. Vladimirs wasn't rehabilitated yet, but I was invited to this lecture by the *Shakhmaty* magazine editor, Latvian master Nikolai Zhuravlev. For the first time in years, I heard the beloved name that was getting recalled. I was grateful to Zhdanov for his bravery. After the lecture, on the way home, I even cried, it was so painful. Yet again, the old question haunted me, "Why?"

I learned at the lecture that Zhuravlev's brother apparently heard that Petrovs worked in the Perm logging camp, a tree fell on him and crushed him to death. A camp guard who remembered Petrovs was still alive. I wanted to go to Perm. The search had started. I wrote a letter to the camp, not even knowing if it still existed, but got no reply. I still can't get rid of my naivete sometimes. Very soon, I heard another rumor – that Petrovs served his time, 10 years, got released and died of a heart attack shortly before his departure to Riga.

I can't think even for a minute that he's still alive and hasn't revealed himself – he loved his family too much for that. But I checked and rechecked, sent inquiries... You could go mad from all those searches and research.

I don't know, Volodya, where your grave is, and I won't likely ever learn that. Is it covered by sand, or encased in ice, or maybe you never underwent any "correction" in the Gulag Archipelago and died in a cell of some Stalinist prison? Let this book, the memories of you, be a headstone and the flowers I lay on your nameless grave.

God rest you, dear Volodya. Let your bright chess star shine brightly and never fade!

My parents also suffered through much cold and hunger. Can this all really be described, put into words? The human language is too poor for that.

The doctor served his time in Vyatlag, miraculously survived and was sent to a settlement in the Krasnoyarsk Krai. My mother took an unimaginable path through the Far North. She worked as a fisher, starved, froze, did impossible work, repenting for her "sins" against the state. She finally managed to reunite with her husband and, after much turmoil, got back to Latvia to see me in 1947. Of course, they had almost no clothes or shoes, looked unrecognizably older, and their health was ruined. The doctor suffered from a stomach ulcer.

They had to start their life anew. But after a long, harrowing separation, we were together again and infinitely happy. Nikolajs Vasilyevich got a doctor's job in Tukums. They had a small studio apartment in a hospital building, and my mom poured herself into decorating it. She would constantly hammer something, sew something, make something. She shone with happiness. She especially loved the marketplace – walking around, looking at the food items that she hadn't seen for years, even without buying anything. We were rather limited in our means, and we had to make sure we had the money for necessities.

I worked as a university teacher in Riga, and my daughter was reunited with her grandparents again, who loved her infinitely and surrounded her with attention, care and affection that I couldn't give her because I was always busy.

But our happiness didn't last long. The year 1949 came, spelling doom to many thousands of long-suffering Latvians. More arrests and deportations followed. In 1941, they wanted to destroy the intelligentsia and empty the cities, but now the sword of Damocles swung over the village dwellers. They needed to devastate and ravage the village, uproot all the peasantry, liquidate the households. They said that they were deporting kulaks. But what kulaks could have remained in the republic after Soviet rule was restored?! All wealthy landlords had already been deported in 1941, their possessions nationalized, and the peasants sent to collective farms.

Repressions also hit those who dared to survive in camps or exile. They endured, no matter what. They weren't broken and destroyed, they were working again, and it seemed that the authorities couldn't tolerate that.

This happened on 13th January (the Old Style New Year). I happily traveled to Tukums to see my parents, brought many bags and sacks of food, anticipating the tasty meat dumplings my mom promised to make and seeing the friends she invited. We were bustling in the kitchen, then I set the table. A sudden ring of the doorbell made me shudder. "The guests are rather early," I thought. I ran to open the door. Three men in blue peaked caps stood before me. They politely asked if the doctor lived here and whether he was home. Like in 1941, he was in the hospital. They sent for him and went to the kitchen to meet my mom. They brought the doctor and told him to gather his things. I remember one of the men saying, "Well, doctor, you are in trouble – you'll have to travel again." I had the thought that those healthy, young, fit guys were eyeing the small, hunched old man in a white coat that he forgot to remove in hospital with pity. They probably imagined that an "enemy of the people" would look different. And then everything repeated as before. They gave them some time to gather their belongings. However, they didn't search the home or hurry my parents. The men sat in silence and smoked. My parents didn't need much time to gather their simple, meager possessions, but they had nothing to pack them in. My mother, panicking, started stuffing her belongings into a blanket. Then one of our friends turned up. They allowed him to run home to get a sled and help pack. I couldn't do anything – I stood in a corner, petrified, hugging my daughter tightly. There was only a single thought in my brain: "Will they take Marina too? I won't give her away, never! If they try, I'll kill them." But my daughter wasn't on the list this time. I was relieved. What more do I remember about that day? Probably nothing. The only other thing that shocked me was my parents' calmness – no tears, no heartbreaking goodbyes. They were totally docile, feeling that everything was inevitable.

My poor old parents were led away. The sack with their belongings was put on the sled – there was no truck or "black raven" outside: the Internal Affairs office was within walking distance, they said. Our friend pulled the sled. I barely managed to get my terrified daughter to sleep, and then I couldn't move – I sat the whole night on the sofa, my legs curled under me. I had no thoughts, no feelings, no tears. I was completely numb, empty, apathetic. In the morning, I ran to the Internal Affairs office. But my parents weren't there – they had already been sent to Riga. I searched high and low in Riga – the Internal Affairs office, the NKVD, the prison... Someone (I don't remember who) said that there was a transfer post at Skirotava station, and the next train would depart from there.

I discovered that my parents were at the transfer post. I filed a request to visit them to give them warm clothes and food. I was allowed to meet them in a checkpoint cabin. My parents weren't so calm and collected anymore – there were tears, and despair, and the pain of separation. I promised that I would come to see them as soon as I learned where they are. My mother, of course, protested vehemently, asked me not to do that. Then they were led away...

I remember that it was very cold. It was getting late. I asked the guards when the train was scheduled to depart, and they said, in the morning. I waited, but got so cold after a few hours that I decided to go to the nearest friend's house and get a bit warmer. But by the time I got back to the station, the train had already departed. They lied to me... Again, I couldn't say goodbye to my family on their way to Calvary. I've tried to find that place near the station many times since then, but I never managed to – everything got rebuilt, no trace of it was left.

The "Conquest" of Siberia

Not long ago *[in 1989]*, a monument was erected at Skirotava station, so that nobody would forget the place and the time when thousands of Latvian citizens were sent to experience pain and suffering. Many of them never returned to their homeland. I couldn't view the song "...I don't know any other country where man breathes so freely" as anything more than mockery, humiliation, sacrilege. After my parents' deportation, it took a lot of strength for me to start living, working, existing again. Everything seemed like a nightmare. I would recall Akhmatova's lines many times:

I've got a lot of work to do today:
I need to kill my memory thoroughly,
I need my soul to petrify,
I need to learn to live again...

With every day, I became more resolute in my decision to drop everything I did in Riga and go to find my parents. But I had to wait for them to contact me. I prayed to God every day that my father wouldn't be separated from my mother. I started to plan my departure, to make the necessary steps.

Soon, everything was decided for me. I was called to the special department of the university and told that since my parents were repressed, and I had hidden that, I had no right to work in the university anymore. Was I supposed to run to them straight away and happily recount the events? They at least magnanimously allowed me to resign from work "on my own accord". I was so relieved. Goodbye, Riga! I had no hesitations...

No amount of arguments, persuasion or warnings from my friends helped. I would just cover my ears and refuse to listen to anybody. Soon, I got a message from my parents – they were together, settled in Krasnoyarsk Krai, in a taiga village called Aban in Dzerzhinsky district. I acted frantically. I drew on new strength and energy from somewhere. Of course, I hadn't thought many things through, which I later realized numerous times. It never occurred to me to do something with my flat – sell it, swap it, register it as mine somehow. I just took my suitcases, asked my friends to sell the remaining furniture and went off to "conquer" Siberia with my daughter. I was still young and overconfident in my strength, in my education... Of course I'll be fine!

A lot of friends came to see me off at the station. Many cried, but I was happy and carefree, as though I was going on some recreational trip. Oh, youth! I hadn't informed my parents of my arrival to avoid further warnings and discouragement. I appeared like a bolt from the blue in June 1949. Aban was 80 km away from the town of Kansk, through which the Far Eastern Railway passed. Internal exiles were forbidden from living any closer.

I won't describe our happy meeting. We were together again, happy again. I bought them a little two-room house, spent the whole summer with them, and used up all my money. I couldn't find any work in the village, and so, leaving my daughter with her grandparents, I went to Kansk to "seek my fortune". That's when the hardships really started; everything I hadn't thought of, hadn't foreseen, hadn't calculated, showed up. I was totally unprepared for the new life. The winter was coming, but I had no felt boots, no warm cap, no clothes necessary to counter the freezing Siberian weather. My only warm clothes were a light sealskin coat and boots on 7-centimeter heels.

When the autumn rains started, it turned out that the roof in the house I had rented was leaky. I had to put a basin at the foot of the bed and pour the water out of the window every half an hour. It was then that a thought first occurred in my head, which I then carried with me throughout my life: "Hold on, to thin air if needed, but hold on!" Everything drove me to despair – especially the fact that I couldn't find a job to match my professional training. Technical colleges and schools needed teachers, I knew several languages to boot, but as soon as it came to job questionnaires, I got rejected for various excuses. At first, I tried to hide the fact that my parents were in exile, but this was not even the main thing that put the officials off – the main reasons were that my degrees were from Riga and that I had spent all my life in Latvia, including under German occupation *[in Tukums, staying with family friends]*. I had to openly explain everything – that I had come from Riga to Siberia for a reason, and my love for this beautiful region was not it.

Losing all hope of finding a proper teaching job, I decided to fight for survival with my musical and ballet skills which I had acquired in my youth. Oh, I had so many jobs! I taught dance, I was an art director in a labor colony, I played the piano in movie theaters between showings, I worked as a choir conductor in a club. I lacked a lot of knowledge and had to learn on the job. Finally, I managed to get a music position in several nursery schools, and when a music school opened in the town, I taught piano and history of music there.

Suddenly, a journalist appeared in Kansk in search of Petrovs' photos. I carried the album, the box with the amber chess set and two cups (one was the brilliancy prize in Kemeri) with me everywhere. I took them to the bomb shelter every time during the war. I gave the journalist nothing. These were my only mementos of Volodya's chess life.

Life gradually changed for the better. I pined for my parents, but they were only allowed to move to Kansk and live with me after Stalin's death. Ten years passed by – no, flew by in Siberia! The doctor was never allowed to work again. During that time, I married Anatolijs Georgievich Matis, a former architecture student from Latvian University who was deported together with his mother and sister on 14th June 1941. He spent some time with my mother in the Far North. His father died in the Solikamsk camp in 1942. Fate brought us together in Kansk, and we had a daughter, Margarita. I won't describe my life in Siberia in much detail. It wasn't that different from the life of exiles. The only difference was that I was a free citizen among all the "slaves", the exiles, a "white sheep" of sorts, even though I felt no difference in social status. Everyone treated me as though I was on a special settlement too, a "dissident", to apply a modern term. Life only became easier after the death of the tyrant, Stalin.

During the Thaw years, I managed to secure the doctor's rehabilitation. I remember that day in 1957. He went to receive his free citizen's passport. He came back, put it on the table and said, "Now I can go freely to the next world with a clean passport." We decided to celebrate that seminal day. My mom went to a kiosk to buy something, and the doctor died within an hour – his poor, tired heart couldn't stand it anymore. Dr. Nikolajs Vasilyevich Lobovikovs was buried with a clean passport. My mother was only released from exile in 1959, and I brought her to Riga. She was already ill and died soon after. Thank God she was buried in her homeland. My poor daughter Marina is also buried there – it seems I couldn't protect her after all, and life in Siberia broke her.

I could write a whole book about the people I met in Siberia. Such a diverse lot! Professors, doctors, lawyers, artists, former ministers and their wives. There were people of various ethnicities – Volga Germans, Crimean Tatars, Georgians, Jews, even a Japanese POW, who was a former mayor of Tokyo. Everyone was brought together by their common bitter fate.

My family life with Anatolijs in Riga didn't last long. We divorced...

Did I regret my actions? My daughter's reproaches stung very painfully. No, I didn't regret them, even though there were some moments of weakness. I wept secretly. At such moments, I remembered Vertinsky's song "The Ball of God", probably because I – I don't know why I did that – brought my beautiful evening dress which I purchased in Paris to Siberia.

There were no balls held in this sleepy town,
There weren't even any decent carriages.
Years went by, you have faded, and your dress did too,
Your marvelous dress – Maison La Valette.

So much for brightening up my parents' life...

Shortly before my departure, I was called to the Internal Affairs office in Kansk. They showed me some photos of people I didn't know. Among other things, they asked me what the lapel pin on Volodya's suit jacket was (the

Lomonosov Grammar School logo). Incredibly, even there, thousands of kilometers from Riga, they had Petrovs' student photo in a case file (either his or mine). They gave it to me, saying nonchalantly, "The dead don't interest us." It happened in 1959...

"God Bless Us For a Free Life!"

Finally, I would like to think about the following question: should we really revisit this horrible past? Isn't it time to forget what happened half a century ago? I discussed this topic with many people with similar experiences, who expressed their desire to erase everything from their memory, to leave the old wounds alone, to forget everything and live for today. They are probably right in their own way. I've tried numerous times to do the same, but I couldn't. I won't live for much longer, but no matter how little time I still have, I tell myself and my grandchildren, "Live and remember." But, remembering the past and looking into the future, we should constantly repeat, "God bless us

Do I have the right to be silent? About what it was like, how it began? I try to interpret events objectively. While, from the Christian point of view, I should forgive everything that took place in plain sight of millions, it is nevertheless impossible to comprehend the full absurdity of what happened. So instead I live and suffer in contradictions

Petrovs' sole child, Marina Vladimirovna. She was two-and-a-half when her father disappeared from her life forever. Did she remember the image of her father, his eyes full with endless love? It's hard to say. But she carried the certainty that he was innocent throughout her life

for a free life!" Throughout my life, I was affected by the Roman law postulate, "A slave born of a slave is a slave." Our democratic, free country still seems to remember that.

And another thing. During those years, my worldview and attitude to the existing political system was shaped definitively and irrevocably. Every day, a protest against lawlessness, human rights violations, abuses and injustice in society burned brighter in my heart. I felt the need to fight, and I'm thankful to my Siberian years for that. Many, many years later these seeds that germinated in the Siberian soils led me to the ideals of the academician and human rights activist Andrei Dmitrievich Sakharov. I had the honor of meeting him, and I keep his autograph as a sacred relic...

When the ex-world champion Euwe first came to Moscow after the war, he started asking around about his friend, Grandmaster Petrovs. When? Where? Why? He got an answer from the Czech master Opocensky: "If the Russians imprisoned such a strong grandmaster, it's clear to everyone that Petrovs did have some sins on his soul." Euwe replied sharply, "I think that Petrovs' only sin was belonging to the Latvian people!"

Afterword by Vladimir Dedkov and Olga Sorokina

We found a Soviet-era cardboard folder with the ribbons torn off in 2007, seven years after the death of our grandmother Galina Mikhailovna Petrova-Matisa. We found it by chance, in a wall cabinet. After leafing through a few pages, we realized that these were materials for the book our grandmother had talked so much about.

There were 309 sheets of typewritten text that included games, tables and space for diagrams – the result of our grandmother's joint work with Andris Fride, journalist and son of the Latvian chess player Janis Fride, thanks to whom many of Petrovs' games survived.

These were materials about our grandfather, the chess player Vladimirs Mikhailovich Petrovs. Had circumstances been just a bit different, we would have never known the story of the life, love and tragic death of our grandfather, and we wouldn't have been able to tell our children and readers about him.

We knew that our grandmother had worked on a book together with Fride for several years, but she wouldn't tell us much about its contents. She only answered tersely, "About Petrovs."

Our family never discussed our repressed grandfather in Soviet times in the presence of kids, and everything we knew about him was limited to scattered phrases we overheard during rare family feasts. For instance, we once heard that our grandfather "rotted in a dungeon", and we told that to a neighbor, a boy. Afterwards, he threatened us numerous times that he would tell everyone in school about that, even though, like me, he didn't understand what that even meant.

The only things the grown-ups didn't hide from us were that I *[Vladimir Dedkov]* was named Vladimir in his memory, and that he was a chess player. They also kept our grandfather's *Bierzipfel*, promising to give it to me if I behaved well, two silver cups and the carved box with a chess set encrusted with amber. But they didn't keep it on display, and after I had once held the box in my hands, they hid all the relics away altogether. They apparently decided that I didn't deserve the *Bierzipfel*, even after I grew up, so I only got to look at it closely after our grandmother's death.

We also knew nothing about our mother's difficulties with education and work.

I did like chess in my childhood, but I was a restless, mischievous kid, so I quit playing rather quickly – on the level of "e2-e4, e7-e5, and then somehow get to checkmate or, if really unlucky, stalemate". Only after turning 25 did I truly start to understand and love this great game. Back then, however, the most important thing for me was to play quickly (this brought better results – perhaps I inherited my grandfather's love of blitz), because my goofy friends were waiting around the corner, where the street and adventures awaited us. Even during the schools team city championship on Smilsu Street, when I played board 1 for my school, chess still took a back seat in my mind. The most important things for me were fuses – everything that had to do with unscrewing the electric fuses that were located outside the apartment back then. Oh, the Old Riga citizens were so unlucky that I found the key that opened fuse boxes exactly at that time...

As we studied the folder's contents, we came to realize that the information about our grandfather's love for chess was not full: there were too few games from the Latvian championships, from tournaments played in the USSR, and, what's most important, our grandfather's last years remained completely unknown. We found some additional information online: several obscure games by our grandfather that were not in the big databases, one of them with the Hungarian player Fazekas who played for England, some photos of our grandfather from the Margate international tournament in England, and annotated games from the 12th Soviet Championship. But the biggest discoveries were the articles by the journalist and publicist Sergey Voronkov, thanks to whom our grandmother met the Czech writer Mirek, who was the last person known to have seen our grandfather at Lubyanka. From these articles, I learned that the book co-authored by Andris Fride and our grandmother was submitted to the Fizkultura and Sport publishing house way back in 1990, and that it was half-ready for publication, but never saw the light of day. Voronkov keeps the half-edited work in his archive, and he regrets that this interesting information hadn't been published yet.

...And so, all the texts were typed and digitized – with tables, diagrams, photos. But we thought that too few personal memories of our grandmother had been included in that manuscript, and she was only rarely mentioned as Petrovs' widow. So we decided to read through all the hand-written recollections of our grandmother again. Thankfully, when my handwriting was still developing, I imitated my grandmother's style of writing some letters, which made the task of deciphering her "scrawl" much easier. Some notes contained short questions on the book – perhaps it was the working plan: what more to write, what shouldn't be missed.

As an example, here are a few short phrases that never got developed further (and now, there's nobody to ask and expand them):

He considered Steinitz the greatest genius.
He brought a Palekh box and a diamond ring from the USSR.
Krumins was the only one who tried to do anything...

In Gorky, he met Diy [my godfather, Diy Nazarovich Dmitriev. – V. D.]. When Volodya talked about us, his eyes filled with tears – he worried about me and Marina so much.

Volodya wanted us to spend the first New Year's Day as a married couple alone together. We went to Schedrovo. A fir tree in the forest...

During the game against Thomas, he read a letter and got into time trouble.

I knew nothing about chess, but I knew that Volodya was unhappy to play black. Does this mean that he played worse with black?

Our grandmother wrote, "My memories about Petrovs cannot be embedded into Fride's text – he writes about the development of chess in Latvia. My recollections are purely personal, there's probably a lot of emotion and sentimentalism. And how should the book be called? *Chess Life in Latvia? The Development of Latvian Chess?* I'll call it *A Star Prematurely Extinguished*, in memory of my husband V. M. Petrovs."

Anyway, we decided against publishing a huge book about our grandfather's chess life out of our own pockets – Fride by then had already published a book in 2004 in America, but without our grandfather's life story and our grandmother's memories. So we decided to concentrate solely on that.

Thanks to fate and everyone who helped with writing this book. By working on it, we have managed to fill, at least partially, the unforgivable blank spot in our family history. We felt as though we were looking into our grandfather's eyes.

Way back, in 1942, my grandfather sent his last ever photo to Riga with a fellow chess player, and he said to him, "I feel I won't see my family anymore, so let me look at them at least from the photo..."

Grandfather, you haven't seen just your wife and daughter – you have seen your grandchildren and great-grandchildren as well.

Thank you, grandfather and grandmother. May your memory be eternal!

Riga, 2008